Advance Praise for
The COURAGE Code

Leisse Wilcox's *The COURAGE Code* is a bold, data-driven, and life-tested guide to emotionally intelligent leadership in the AI era. With humor, heart, and hard-won wisdom, she delivers seven (plus one!) transformative strategies that empower you to lead with confidence, authenticity, and integrity. In the Age of AI, this book helps you build your competitive advantage on leading people. Read it, live it, lead with it!

—Evan Piekara - Nestlé Director of Change Management, Author

•

An easy-to-read, insightful, practical playbook for what true authentic leadership looks like. Leisse weaves her insights through real-life stories, practical tools, and ten-minute activities to really make COURAGE stick.

—Lesley Hawkins - Former VP Retail, Adidas,
Keynote Speaker, Consultant, and Podcast Host

•

Within *The COURAGE Code*, Leisse has ensured there is one (okay . . . way more than just one!) compelling fact, insight, experience, or lesson learned on absolutely every single page. What is even more valuable, though, is how easy it is to remember the COURAGE Code and practically apply it to any number of situations. Whether you read from cover to cover, or pick and choose those chapters that meet you where you are in a given moment, adding her advice to your own commitment consistently drives you forward on your journey of personal growth. *The COURAGE Code* belongs on the reading list for all leaders.

—Deborah Antenore, Hydro One Human Resources Leader

•

Another fantastic read from Leisse! She has a true gift for distilling essential leadership skills into clear, practical, and easy-to-apply insights. I especially appreciated the tips, tricks, and real-world examples that help leaders not only "get it" but also stay grounded in the core foundations of leadership and communication. At the heart of it all is one powerful theme—COURAGE. A must-read for anyone looking to elevate their leadership journey.

–Tara Talbot, Former WildBrain EVP Global Talent,
Strategic Advisor, CHRO

•

The COURAGE Code is a refreshing and insightful take on leadership that blends humor, storytelling, and practical advice into a compelling read. Leisse Wilcox masterfully uses wit and relatable anecdotes to deliver clear, actionable strategies for leaders who want to be more effective in the way they communicate, connect, and lead with authenticity.

Whether you're a seasoned executive or starting your leadership journey, this book offers valuable tactics to help you communicate with clarity, build trust, and lead with confidence. Equal parts entertaining and instructive, The COURAGE Code is a practical guide for those looking to grow their leadership impact while staying true to who they are.

The COURAGE Code isn't your run-of-the-mill leadership book—it's smarter, funnier, and way more human. Leisse weaves together real-life stories and practical advice in a way that makes you nod, laugh, and immediately think, "I can use this."

–Dr. Danielle Paes - Former Chief Pharmacist Officer,
Canadian Pharmacists' Association

•

As a long-time leader in talent management, I'm always searching for books that deliver both inspiration and practicality. Too often, they're theory-heavy with little real-world value. *The COURAGE Code* breaks that mold. Structured like a "choose your own adventure," it gives leaders clear building blocks to focus on what matters most. Written in a humorous, conversational style, it's packed with sharp insights and actionable frameworks. With real-life examples and practical tips, it's concise, relatable, and adaptable. *The COURAGE Code* is more than just a read; it's a practical pact. It's the kind of book that makes you reflect and rethink how you approach tough situations. Most importantly, it hands you the tools to act with courage in your own way.

–Daniella van Weringh - Danone Senior Leader,
Talent, Culture and Leadership

•

For anyone looking to invest in their personal growth and development, *The COURAGE Code* does a brilliant job of highlighting the key communication strategies needed to shift your mindset and focus on making impact through actions. Leisse shares her expertise and experiences through candid and relatable storytelling and practical approaches. This is a perfect resource for anyone looking to upskill the way they show up every day.

–Manisha Mistry - CSA Group Senior Leader,
Safety, Inclusion and Sustainability

•

The
COURAGE
Code

**7 Communication Strategies
to Change the Way We
Work, Live, and Lead**

The COURAGE Code

7 Communication Strategies to Change the Way We Work, Live, and Lead

LEISSE WILCOX

The COURAGE Code: 7 Communication Strategies to Change the Way We Work, Live, and Lead

2025 fEMPOWER Press Trade Paperback Edition
Copyright © 2025 LEISSE WILCOX

Published in Canada, for Global Distribution by fEMPOWER Publications
www.fempower.pub | For more information email: media@fempower.pub

ISBN trade paperback: 9781998721023
ISBN hardback: 978-1-998721-32-0
eBook: 9781998721191

To order additional copies of this book: media@fempower.pub

"Courage is grace under pressure."

–Ernest Hemingway

About the Cover

The cover art was created and designed by Grey Wilcox, my twelve-year-old (at the time) daughter. I wanted an image that would feel like a spark—a visual representation of the powerful energy and transformation this book embodies. Her fine art skills and creativity perfectly captured that, and I am so proud to feature her artwork front and center.

Each color was intentionally chosen to reflect the journey and the essence of the book's message:

Red represents the courage to take bold steps in leadership and life, fueling the fire of transformation.

Blue brings a sense of calm, trust, and integrity, foundational elements for authentic leadership.

Gold shines with the promise of success and achievement, as well as the wisdom gained through resilience.

Purple symbolizes creativity and transformation, a nod to the creative power we all have to shape our futures, even in the face of challenges.

White offers clarity, representing new beginnings and the fresh perspectives that come when we step into our power.

This cover is not only a reflection of the personal and professional journey I hope to inspire you to take but also a tribute to the spark of creativity that is central to transformation. Having my daughter's art play such a central role in the visual storytelling of this book makes it all the more meaningful.

For MCG: May you always find, have, and *use* the courage you need, and for JJM, who constantly reminds me to have, find, and use mine.

ILYASM.

Contents

Intro

I'm sitting at a long table, one made of pulling several small tables together. It's our annual corporate Christmas lunch in the upstairs "event space" at a downtown Italian restaurant. If you can get past the weird smell of old fryer grease and the fact that none of us respects our boss, it's kind of a nice outing.

Human Resources has brought in a celebrity graphologist[1] (a.k.a. a handwriting analysis expert) as our entertainment—and if you just rolled your eyes like I did when I first heard this, I feel you; stay with me.

Over plates of antipasti and eggplant parmesan, watered-down drinks, and the awkward moments that come from having not-work-related-but-also-not-too-personal conversations around the table, we wait as Andy[2], the celebrity graphologist, strides to the head of the table holding tiny squares of paper and a handful of clear blue Bic pens.

After a brief introduction that attempts to establish his legitimacy and the credibility of graphology as a science, he hands out the paper and pens, asking us to pass them down until everyone on our team has one. He then asks us to write out the same sentence ten times without overthinking it, something like "the quick brown fox jumped over the lazy dog," plus the date. He is very clear that we are not to write our names.

When we're finished, we gather them up at random, shuffle them around a little, and hand them back; he's had his back turned this whole time to instill a sense of objectivity. I have to say that between the jokes he's been cracking, and his humble showmanship, my inner cynic is softening a little, and I'm even a little excited to see what happens next.

Showtime.

Andy does his own paper shuffle, then chooses a slip at random. While looking at the handwriting sample in front of him, and analyzing the pressure of the pen, the direction of the tilt, the size of loops, and the distance of the dots over the i's[3], Andy begins to describe our senior editor to a T:

"This person is highly creative, with a killer attention to detail; they have a hard exterior with a huge heart and have overcome a lot. Very dependable, very funny—and more extroverted than they let on."

"Ohhhhh, that's JENNA!" we shout. "No question!" He holds up the writing sample for Jenna to verify. We clap, and soften, realizing that maybe Andy isn't the idiot we'd all (cough, *I*) expected.

He continues, analyzing one personality at a time as the rest of us gleefully cheer him on, trying to flag the waiter for another round.

And then it happens.

Andy picks out the next sample from the stack and his face changes. "Wow," he says, squinting. "This person is incredibly sensitive . . . and has huge emotional intelligence." He squints again, holding the paper closer, then further away. "This person is a great communicator and understands how to really reach people," he says. "Very good listener too." Andy continues to describe this person using details so similar to my own life experience that it feels eerie.

"It's *Leisse!*" my manager exclaims. The whole table turns their heads toward me, nodding, bright-eyed, as I sit, overwhelmed at trying to process that this description is my entire personality, making me feel like I'm watching a Netflix docuseries about my life I didn't know was being made. I feel seen in a way I don't think I ever have before.

I don't know exactly what happened next, but I do know something about this experience changed me. It allowed me to see inside myself and put together the seemingly random pieces of a puzzle I'd been trying to solve for an embarrassingly long time.

Where IQ measures your intelligence and aptitude for learning, EQ measures your ability to recognize, understand, and regulate not only your own emotions but also the emotions of others. This allows you to effectively communicate, solve problems, make decisions, and build strong relationships via empathy and self-awareness. These were all skills I knew I had—but hadn't yet had the language or life experience to identify how valuable they were.

- **SELF-AWARENESS:** Understanding your own emotions and how they affect your behavior
- **SELF-REGULATION:** Managing your emotions effectively, especially in challenging situations
- **MOTIVATION:** Having a drive to achieve goals and persevere through setbacks
- **EMPATHY:** Having the ability to understand and share the feelings of others
- **SOCIAL SKILLS:** Building and maintaining positive relationships through effective communication

Emotional intelligence, or emotional quotient (EQ), has become a buzzword in recent years, because frankly?

Robots are taking over the world.

And I'm only half kidding.

Now that we are firmly in the "who let the genie out of the bottle" era of AI, automating everything from scheduling, copywriting, data analysis, and even artwork, the one thing we can't automate is relationships. In fact, studies[4] show that as automation increases, the demand for interpersonal skills rises dramatically—because the human element becomes the differentiator.

Leadership and communication in the AI Revolution demands a renewed focus on emotional intelligence and relationship building, something that is going to feel wildly uncomfortable to a hell of a lot of leaders.

Why?

Because generations of past (and current) leaders were taught to prioritize:

- Ego over empathy
- Winning over well-being
- Profit over people
- Results over relationships

Research[5] shows that emotional intelligence is the *number one* leadership skill for success, yet in our tech-obsessed society, the foundational skills of great leadership—empathy, resilience, and communication—are slipping through the cracks.

We are facing a crisis shaping the future of leadership:

Declining Leadership Resilience: In a rapidly changing world, 60 percent of leaders report feeling overwhelmed by uncertainty and change.[6] (*Harvard Business Review*)

Work-Life Integration Challenges: 57 percent of parents struggle to balance work demands with meaningful family connections.[7] (Newswire Canada)

AI's Impact on Leadership: The World Economic Forum ranks emotional intelligence among the top 10 skills leaders need to stay relevant in an automated world.

Intergenerational Communication Gaps: With five generations collaborating in the workplace, effective communication and shared understanding have never been more crucial.

There's no question that AI and other emerging tech can be partners and tools to leverage; returning to the core of what makes us human is what will allow the leaders who get it to stay relevant, and it is something no amount of tech or app updates can resolve—it's a people problem that takes *genuine courage* from *real people* to solve.

And while "emotional intelligence" may feel like a corporate buzzword up there with "synergy," "bandwith," and "low hanging fruit," let me assure you that having the skillset to *communicate* with emotional intelligence is a classic—and isn't going away anytime soon.

My experience as Chief People Officer of a leading infrastructure company, in addition to my background in Executive Performance and Organizational Development coaching and being a best-selling author, award-winning keynote speaker, cancer survivor, and single mom of three (ergo the life experiences that put the COURAGE Code to the test) has provided me with unique insights into what it takes to build resilience, authenticity, and adaptability in today's chaotic world.

I have more than twenty years' experience in leadership development, corporate training, and keynote speaking, as well as cultivating emotional intelligence in myself and thousands of others. I've had the privilege of working with leaders across the globe, helping them navigate the complexities of modern leadership—at work, home, and life.

Through the COURAGE Code framework, I offer practical, actionable strategies grounded in real-life experience and data-driven research.

The COURAGE Code highlights critical trends shaping the future of leadership: it is a practical framework that equips leaders with the tools to navigate uncertainty and drive meaningful impact in their organizations and personal lives using simple, powerful strategies to change the way we show up at work, home, the boardroom, in presentations, and even on LinkedIn:

C – Choose Confidence (Permission to Show Up)

O – Own Who You Are (Lead with Authenticity)

U – Unshakeable Resilience (Powerfully Navigate Uncertainty)

R – Radical Self-Awareness (Get Out of Your Own Way)

A – Aligned Action (Define What "Enough" Feels Like)

G – Growth Through Communication (Kind + Clear + Direct = Trust)

E – Execute with Integrity (Close the Say-Do Gap)

Easy, right?

#lolz

It is that simple—it is that complicated.

The COURAGE Code is designed to give you access to the not-so-soft skills required to activate, elevate, and accelerate your own emotional intelligence through next-level communication skills.

Whether you are a:

- Corporate leader / HR professional seeking strategies to build high-performing, human-centered workplaces
- Business owner / Entrepreneur looking to lead with courage and inspire your team to adapt and grow
- Working parent balancing leadership at home and work, doing it all at the same time, making it look easy while white-knuckling your grip on the illusion of perfection trying to foster connection everywhere you go
- Founder / Emerging leader developing essential communication skills to stay competitive and relevant in an evolving landscape
- Woman in a male-dominated field doubling down on shoring up her confidence and executive presence for the "end" of DEI and the beginning of the Great Wealth Transfer . . .

. . . *I wrote this for you.*

In today's economy, where performance is judged by both impact and influence, courageous communication is no longer optional—it's a competitive advantage. The COURAGE Code will equip you with actionable takeaways to develop your leadership potential and thrive in an ever-evolving professional landscape at any age or stage of your career. It is industry-agnostic, and it provides a road map to future-proof leadership ensuring that relationships, authenticity, and resilience remain at the forefront of success.

Each of the strategies in this book are data-driven and life-tested. I've used them with my corporate clients from junior to senior level and C-suite, with my entrepreneurial and founder clients, my husband, my *three daughters*, and myself. Every tip, trick, and strategy in this book has been field-tested—in my work, in my life, and yes, even at home with my three kids, and I can say with 100 percent certainty that if you decide to adopt these strategies as a daily practice in your work, home, and leadership lives, *you will get results.*

Period.

If it were easy, everyone would do it.

You are *not* everyone; just by you reading this I know that you are one of the 15 percent who commits to their own development.

I am the invisible cheerleader high-fiving you from afar.

I've made it as easy as possible by ending the chapters with actionable takeaways to activate, elevate, and accelerate what you read here and turn it into action. In addition, you'll find a few game-changing prompts to make these communication strategies your new go-to.

Like, now.

So.

My friend? *The COURAGE Code* is not just another leadership book—it's a guide to mastering the single most important skill of the AI era: human connection.

**Ready to change
the way we work, live
and lead?**

Let's go.

How to Use This Book

We don't have time to be inspired. Am I right?

We need practical, tactical tools and strategies that we can start using *this afternoon* to make a measurable impact on how we work, live, and lead.

Gone are the days when business and leadership books had to be 300-page ivory tower tomes packed with jargon and theory.

This book was designed with one clear intention:

To meet you where you are.

It's a leadership resource designed for real life, where emotionally intelligent *communication fuels action* to build trust, lead teams, and get results.

On the train, between meetings, in the pick-up line, or with twenty minutes before your next Zoom call, each chapter is intentionally short—on purpose.

You can read this book cover to cover in just over an hour, or dip in and out when you need a specific mindset reset, strategy, or communication tool.

And because leadership doesn't happen in a vacuum, you'll find a dedicated section at the back just for book clubs and group discussions—to help you bring the COURAGE Code into your ERG community, mastermind, and leadership circles in a meaningful, engaging way.

Congratulations on having the COURAGE to be here now.

COURAGE

STRATEGY NO. 1:

C – Choose Confidence

Strategy No. 1:
C – Choose Confidence
(Permission to Show Up)

I come from a huge family, both in quantity (my Oma and Opa had nine children, nineteen grandchildren, and eleven great-grandchildren . . . at the time of publishing) and stature (at five-foot-eight, I am one of the *shortest* in the whole gang).

One of my aunts tells a story about her youngest son who was toddling around at eighteen months in a onesie when a friend of hers visiting for coffee exclaimed, "He's so . . . *macho.*"

My cousin Aaron (now in his late twenties with a whole different clothing aesthetic) today stands at six-foot-five and looks like a blond Disney prince.

No joke.

Aaron was *born* confident and is the *only* exception to this otherwise steadfast rule:

No one is born confident.

There is a misconception, even among top leaders, high performers, and hyper-independent overachievers, that some people are confident, and some are not.

False.

For everyone other than my cousin Aaron, confidence is a choice. It's up to you to choose it daily, and just like going to the gym to get shredded (much like that same cousin o' mine), it's a muscle we flex and build till it's strong enough for us to rely on.

Let me say that again, louder for the cheap seats in the back:

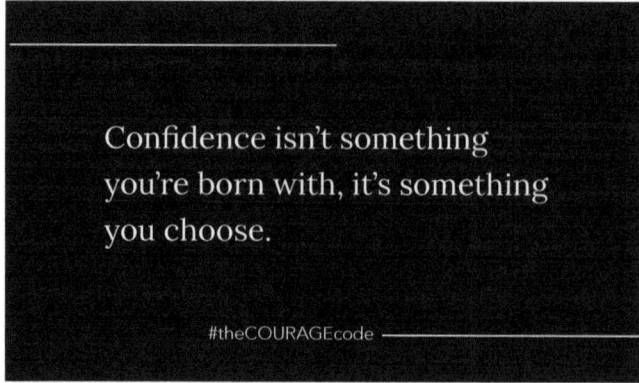

Confidence isn't something
you're born with, it's something
you choose.

#theCOURAGEcode

Whether in leadership, relationships, or personal growth, the decision to show up confidently creates a ripple effect that shapes your entire experience. But too often we wait for external validation before believing in ourselves, when in reality, it starts within.

CONFIDENCE MYTHS VS. TRUTHS	
MYTH	**TRUTH**
Confidence is loud, pushy, and aggressive.	True confidence is understated, clear, kind, and assertive.
Confidence means taking big, bold actions right away.	Confidence grows through small, achievable wins— consistently.
Confidence is constant and unwavering.	Confidence is contextual; it ebbs and flows depending on the situation.
You need to feel confident before taking action.	Taking action is what makes you *feel* confident.

MYTH	TRUTH
Confidence comes after epic success.	Confidence starts with small steps; epic success follows.
Confidence always comes first, then action.	Action often comes first, and confidence builds from there.
Confidence means perfection.	Confidence means making and owning mistakes. You know— being human.
Confidence is for some and not others.	Confidence is available to anyone who wants it, period.

Because we are social creatures who bond with others via comfort, trust, and likeability, we are magnetically drawn to those who exude qualities that make us feel seen, heard, and valued.

We want to feel safe in ourselves and in the presence of others, so anyone who demonstrates that *they* already feel safe and comfortable, and demonstrate that *je ne sais quoi* that makes it easy and fun to be around them, has our immediate attention—and buy-in.

Cult leaders and con artists have known this from the jump.

#awkward

But *unlike* cult leaders and con artists, when we cultivate these skills for good and pair them with values, intention, and moral integrity, we create incredible and context-agnostic relationships with others.

Leaders who can make quick and conscious decisions, who are clear, kind, and direct in their communication, and who make us feel at ease in their presence *know* that showing up with confidence is more likely to earn our trust, inspire us to

> Confidence is the cornerstone
> of leadership.
>
> #theCOURAGEcode

make decisive choices, and allow us to navigate uncertainty with more ease.

A study by the *Harvard Business Review* found that leaders who exhibit confidence are 75 percent more likely to be seen as competent and capable, even when their experience is comparable to their peers.[8] Confidence correlates directly with higher performance, stronger relationships, and greater career advancement opportunities.

This doesn't mean that confident leaders are 100 percent perfect 100 percent of the time. If you've ever read or watched anything by researcher and author Brené Brown, you know the power that lies in our vulnerability and that it is in being *confident enough to be vulnerable* that makes us strong.

Take public speaking for example:

I remember learning in my university social psychology classes that presenters who stumble over a word, or drop one of their papers, or make any number of teeny tiny little human errors—even in front of a large or prestigious crowd—tend to be viewed *more favorably* with the audience.

Kinda takes the pressure off your next presentation, right?

Research shows that people often respond positively to such behaviors because it makes them appear more relatable and authentic, thus fostering empathy and engagement from the audience.[9]

Confidence is more than a mindset—it's a way of being that encompasses authenticity and self-assurance, which we can each convey through our words, actions, tone, and body language. Embracing vulnerability can actually *bolster* confidence, as it allows us to perform less and connect more with our audience, presenting ourselves at our most genuine.

Confidence isn't just the words we use, either: *it's the way we carry and present ourselves at any given moment.* It's how we take up space and truly *own* the room.

I can tell you that when I wear a dress and heels to a keynote or other presentation—even the *nicest* dress with the *most comfortable* heels—*my delivery is sub-par* to when I wear wide-leg, higher-the-waist-the-closer-to-God pants with sneakers and a button-down.

When I dress the part of what I think I *should* look like or wear, a part of me stays focused on what I look like or am wearing—because let's be real: I'm trying hard not to trip, fall, or break an ankle in those heels.

However.

When I dress the part of *what I want* to look like or wear, I feel confident to just be myself: relaxed, powerful, and at ease—and the feedback from the audience is measurably higher.

When we *choose* confidence, we *choose* to feel comfortable or at ease, and it changes how we show up.

Posture:

Our body language[10], energy, and disposition are a walking billboard that speaks more loudly than before we've even opened our mouths.

If our posture is standing or sitting upright with an open stance (shoulders back, arms at ease), we signal self-assurance. If we are hunched over or closed off with arms crossed, it demonstrates a distance or edginess to those around us.

And what's more? We can "act as if" we're *already* confident just by changing our physical stance. The research shows that simply adopting postures or poses of confidence can enhance our own feelings of confidence—while creating an air of confidence in those in our presence.[11]

Power pose, baby.

Eye Contact:

You know the magic moment that happens juuuuust before the first kiss? It's one of the most powerful reminders we have that the eyes truly are the windows to the soul.

Being able to look someone directly in the eyes and hold contact there is a huge power move (. . . *and just a little bit sexy, amiright?*).

Holding eye contact without wavering, especially during moments of conflict or other discomfort, demonstrates presence, authority, engagement, and confidence.

Conversely, avoiding eye contact can be perceived as disinterest or insecurity.[12] I bet you've seen enough true crime documentaries to know that the guilty have a very hard time making eye contact. We convey so much social code through this one seemingly small behavior.

Gestures:

Any other hand-talkers out there? Keep the stemmed wine glasses away from me while I'm mid-conversation. We use our hands to communicate what we're feeling on the inside, anywhere on the spectrum of passion to defeat.

Purposeful or controlled hand movements can emphasize points and convey confidence. What you do with the rest of your body matters to—before, during, or after you've said any words.

Using your hands as an illustration of what you're communicating can be an incredible tool to build trust and engagement—but on the other hand (no pun intended), fidgeting, shuffling, or closed-off gestures like clenched hands/fists, shrugged shoulders, or crossed arms can suggest nervousness or defensiveness.

Grounding yourself to stay physically at ease will help you stay in your assertive confidence.

Facial Expressions:

We all know someone with RBF[13]; unintentionally (and unfairly), they accidentally communicate a standoffishness that the more sensitive among us tend to take personally and assume that person is upset or angry at us.

Tense facial muscles, forced expressions, a frown, furrowed brows, or squinting/overly relaxed eyes can indicate discomfort, which we, in turn, start to internalize or interpret as "not approachable."

On the contrary, someone with a relaxed face, bright open eyes, or a genuine smile almost immediately projects warmth and confidence no matter if we've known them for twenty seconds or twenty years.

All that to say:

Choosing confidence is how you show up and own the room.

Your body language speaks before your mouth does. And while these body language cues are generally associated with confidence, it's important to note that cultural differences can influence their interpretation.

And the wonderful thing is that because this is a learned skill, you can start by simply pretending you are confident by showing up as if you are already confident. "Acting as if" you are already a confident person starts to trick your brain into believing you *are* that confident person—because our brain can't tell the difference between reality and non-reality.

Don't believe me?

Go watch a horror movie alone in the dark and tell me you're not afraid . . . even though you know rationally it's not real.

Acting As If

Ever see the 2008 interview between Oprah and Beyoncé? It's one of my favorite leadership hacks for any client (cough, me) who's facing feelings of momentary inadequacy or not enough-ness and is spiraling into staying small to avoid *doing the thing* because of a lack of confidence.

In the interview, Beyoncé explains that being on stage and dancing, singing, and slaying is something that Beyoncé

Knowles could never do; thus, she created the Sasha Fierce persona, an alter ego she adopts just before going on stage in her heels, lashes, and bodysuit in front of a cheering crowd.

The Beyoncé we see on stage is like a character in a movie:

Sasha Fierce comes out to play during performances to help her overcome shyness and embody a more assertive, fearless version of herself, the version that delivers powerful performances with confidence and energy and wins Grammy awards.

While offstage and in her private life, however, Beyoncé is more reserved and modest.

Folks?

If Queen Bey needs an alter ego, can we all give ourselves permission to do the same?

Creating that alter ego and acting as if we are that person teaches our mind that it's "safe" for us to BE that person. And ever so interestingly, we are able to almost collapse time, closing the gap between who we are now and who we aspire to be in the future.

When we practice showing up as that person, that idealized alter ego of ourself, we kinda just . . . become that person.

How great is that?

Now, it's important to note that *acting as if* is a far cry from *fake it until you make it.*

"Faking it till you make it" requires you to be someone you are not. It's basically a shortcut to inauthenticity and impostor syndrome. "Acting as if" allows you to visualize and tap into more of who you truly are.

Some people call this your future or higher self.

Getting clear on who you really are because of the values you have allows you to create that renewed sense of self and start acting as if you already are that person . . . right here, right now.

I will never forget working with my client Frida, a female executive vice president in the otherwise male-dominated energy sector. Frida wanted to get out of the infinity loop of overthinking and give herself permission to do and feel all the things she wanted to—without constantly stopping to second-guess herself.

Because Frida had always had a little daydream fantasy about having (slash living on) a yacht, she created her alter ego, "Yacht Frida."

We determined that Yacht Frida—the best possible version of herself—was out on the boat, wearing a muumuu, gin and tonic in hand, and felt comfortable, free, and at ease.

Yacht Frida always made decisions from *that* place, not the tense, stressed, over-thinking and people-pleasing habits of the existing Frida herself.

I still get texts from her telling me the kinds of decisions she's made from her alter ego—that now allows her "real" self to show up and lead with more confidence—because she now feels comfortable doing so.

People who attend my workshops and speaking events often say to me, "If I had an ounce of your confidence, I would . . ." I always tell them it is not a natural quality in me but rather something I have practiced.

I grew up in an emotionally and mentally abusive household—and had to actively work at becoming comfortable with simply being myself.

I'll let you in on a little secret (but my children will be SO embarrassed that I'm sharing this with you):

My own alter ego is Paloma van Walraven.

She is poised and put together, channels a Dutch-girl-in-New-York vibe, has the best sense of humor, and is completely unafraid to take bold strides like pitching herself as a speaker for mega events like TED without an "x" and Work Human or cold calling executives at Fortune 500 companies with confidence and ease.

She knows that the best makeup is great skin, buys few things of high quality, and is unfussed by the North American pressure for MORE.

Paloma van Walraven makes decisions from a place of big-picture vision and does not sweat the short-term ups and downs. She owns every room she walks into and is confident she belongs.

The confidence, courage, and self-assuredness that people see in me now is both real *and* a learned skill that I practiced daily, often with the help of channeling Paloma van Walraven at my side. Sometimes I *still* call on her when I'm in the process of any new upward trajectory or transition in my personal or professional life.

This concept of creating an alter ego is a *highly* valuable strategy for individuals looking to enhance their confidence and presence in various aspects of life, such as public speaking, leadership, navigating crises, having a difficult conversation, managing a major change, and other challenging situations.

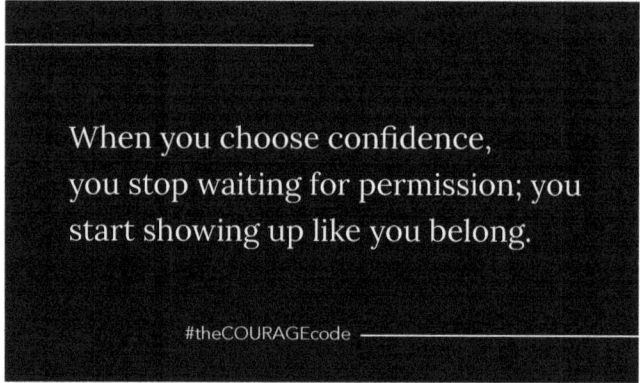

When you choose confidence, you stop waiting for permission; you start showing up like you belong.

#theCOURAGEcode

For 99.999999 percent of the world's population, confidence isn't an innate trait; it's a decision we make that, like a muscle, gets stronger every time we use it.

As a communication strategy, choosing confidence is a powerful tool to demonstrate your leadership prowess before you even say a word, and it's available to each of us at any moment in time.

Listen: There's no one coming to give you confidence, make you confident, or permit you to be confident.

(I think they made a movie about this: something about a yellow brick road and a cowardly lion? I feel like there were ruby-red slippers and flying monkeys . . .)

You are the one who gets to decide if "Choosing Confidence" is a strategy you want to use to change how you work, live, and lead.

COURAGE in Action: Turn Your Insights into Impact

Activate – Make choosing confidence a daily habit. Start small and take note or be aware of how you show up and take up space.

Elevate – Design and step into your alter ego: What are they like? How do they speak, show up, dress, interact, make decisions? Channel a bold, self-assured version of yourself (think *Sasha Fierce*, or *CEO You*) when speaking, presenting, or making decisions.

Accelerate – Embodiment is everything. Communicate like the leader you already are and know you can be simply by showing up as the version of you that has the courage to show up with presence, take up space, and align your body language, tone, and messaging to reflect unwavering confidence.

Game Changers

Want results? Take ten minutes and start here.

WHEN DO YOU FEEL MOST "YOURSELF" AND MOST AT EASE?

What would it look like to bring *that version* of you into your next meeting, conversation, or challenge?

DESIGN YOUR ALTER EGO.

Give them a name, a look, a tone of voice. How would *they* walk into a room today? Practice channeling them for one interaction this week.

AUDIT YOUR BODY LANGUAGE.

What are your go-to postures or expressions in high-pressure situations? Choose one signal (eye contact, stance, facial expression) to shift this week.

WHAT'S ONE SMALL WAY YOU CAN ACT "AS IF" YOU ALREADY ARE THE CONFIDENT VERSION OF YOURSELF?

Choose it. Do it. Repeat tomorrow.

C

COURAGE

Strategy No. 2:
O – Own Who You Are
(Lead with Authenticity)

I'm driving east on the highway, fast, knowing my exit is coming soon.

I have to time it so I can hit my destination without running into anyone I know, and I have to hide the evidence when I'm done. I've only been driving for forty-three minutes, but I have been thinking about this moment for weeks.

As soon as the event I'm speaking at was booked into my calendar, I knew—KNEW—I would have to make this stop and keep it a secret from everyone I know.

My final destination today, coming up on the right? Brace yourself . . .

The Taco Bell drive-through.

I LOVE tacos. I have always been happy to post pics on Instagram of all the cool and authentic taquerias I find and enjoy while traveling—but I have seldomly shared the deeper reality of this taco love affair:

Taco Bell.

Finding the most authentic Mexican tacos in New York and Palm Springs[14] feels cool; upgrading your Crunchwrap Supreme combo to include fries supreme and a diet Pepsi at the drive-through feels . . . *dirty.*

For a long time I kept this food crush to myself, and because I live in Canada, there are so few locations that you really need to be a die-hard fan to know where to find them, outside of the food courts at the mall.

It sounds silly now, but at the time, I was so afraid of being judged or perceived in an otherwise negative way that I kept this part of myself hidden. However. At the first client retreat I hosted, I accidentally let the cat out of the bag and shared this long-held, taco-flavored secret of mine with my clients.

And the result?

Two of the gals there, long-term clients of mine, admitted they shared the same affinity for south-of-the-border deliciousness. We were already pretty close, but I kid you not, this brought us *closer.*

There was something so freeing about feeling comfortable enough to share "all" parts of myself, even in my position as the facilitator of the retreat and long-time coach of these two clients in particular. It sounds bananas to say this out loud, but honestly? The ability to simply own who I am—even the parts I was a little bit ashamed of—built a deeper level of trust and connection through the vulnerability of simply being myself.

True leadership is not about being perfect, it's about being authentic.

> When leaders show up as their true selves, they create an environment where others feel safe to do the same.
>
> #theCOURAGEcode

Not "Authentic™," but genuine, relatable, *show me who you are* authentic.

Authenticity isn't just a buzzword, it's an emotionally intelligent *superpower* that fosters relatability, trust, and influence.

And it pours gasoline on the fire of good communication.

This is not a new concept.

Ralph Waldo Emerson said:

"To be yourself in a world that is constantly trying to make you something else is the greatest accomplishment."

Coco Chanel stated:

"A girl should be two things: who and what she wants."

And taking a more, um, "direct" approach, Frank Zappa declared:

"If you end up with a boring miserable life because you listened to your mom, your dad, your teacher, your priest, or some guy on television telling you how to do your shit, then you deserve it."

No matter which approach to authenticity resonates with you, the truth remains the same:

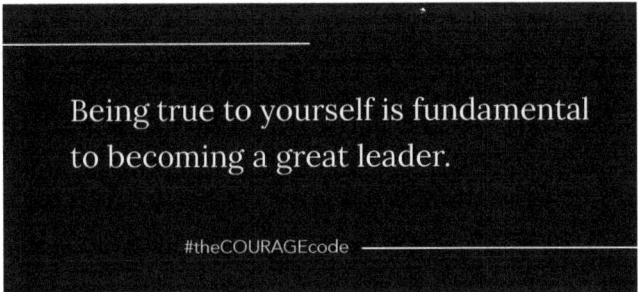

Being true to yourself is fundamental to becoming a great leader.

#theCOURAGEcode

The Role of Authenticity in Communication and Leadership

Authentic leadership is the foundation of emotional intelligence and effective leadership.

When you own who you are, you create deeper connections, inspire trust, and foster meaningful relationships. Owning your identity means leading from a place of alignment—where your values, actions, and words are all in sync.

Being authentic makes you a better leader because it builds trust, influence, and impact—three essential components of effective leadership. Here's how:

Trust & Psychological Safety:

Authentic leaders foster psychological safety, allowing teams to take risks, voice concerns, and innovate without fear of judgment. *Trust fuels high-performance teams.*

Stronger Influence & Connection:

People don't follow titles, they follow people. Authentic leaders cultivate deep, meaningful relationships because they are relatable, human, and real—not just an authority figure. *They inspire through connection, not command.*

Better Decision-Making:

Authenticity means alignment between values and actions. Leaders who know who they are and what they stand for make clear, decisive choices that align with their purpose. *This clarity reduces hesitation, inconsistency, and second-guessing.*

Resilience in Uncertainty:

Authentic leaders don't rely on external validation, they trust their inner compass. This self-trust makes them adaptable and able to pivot without losing their core identity. In times of change or crisis, *authenticity provides stability and direction* because people know what to expect.

Higher Engagement & Loyalty:

When employees see their leader being real—owning mistakes, communicating with clarity, and leading with purpose—they become more engaged and committed. *Authentic leadership creates cultures of ownership where people feel valued* and motivated to contribute.

To put things in perspective?

A *Harvard Business Review* survey found 58 percent of employees trust a stranger on the street more than they do their own boss.[15]

Nuff said.

The demand for authentic leadership is so strong we can taste it. So, how do we make that happen?

This is an inner job.

Owning who you are is an inside job that requires:

Radical Responsibility:

Owning your actions and outcomes without excuses. Owning who you are requires radical responsibility—taking ownership of your choices, actions, and the vision you create for your life and leadership. It's about stepping away from blame and excuses and instead embracing full accountability for shaping your path forward.

Next-Level Self-Awareness:

Understanding who you are at your core, beyond external expectations, allows you to be authentic. Owning who you are requires deep self-trust. It means valuing your own judgment over external validation and resisting the urge to hand over your authority to others.

Especially in industries where women are still underrepresented, owning your strengths unapologetically becomes a quiet act of rebellion—and a bold act of leadership.

Own Your Zone:

Understanding and owning your unique strengths—your genius zone—is key to authentic leadership. No more shrinking to fit. Stepping into your power unapologetically allows you to contribute your best self without dilution. Identify your genius zone—and stay there.

Recognizing your strengths and dedicating yourself to them leads to fulfillment and impact. It takes courage to stay true to what you excel at and to resist the urge to conform to external expectations. Own your zone, and don't apologize for it.

Define Your Values:

Knowing your core values and crafting a vision that aligns with them is essential for leading with authenticity. Your values act as a compass, guiding your decisions and actions with integrity.

As we look ahead to leading Gen Z and Gen Alpha, we know this is going to become an even more valuable quality in leadership. A 2021 study from Ernst & Young found that value wise, *for Gen Z, authenticity is more important than future plans and being rich.*[16]

So, if we want to future-proof our leadership, authenticity isn't optional—it's essential. Getting comfortable to *be* who we are and own the strengths, weaknesses, and picadillos that go along with it are crucial to building an ongoing sense of trust and employee buy-in.

Again, authenticity **isn't about being perfect**—it's about being real, leading with integrity, and aligning actions with values. When you own who you are, you unlock the full potential of your leadership.

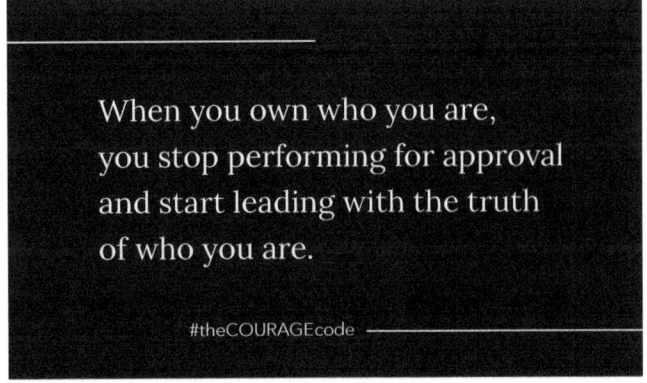

When you own who you are,
you stop performing for approval
and start leading with the truth
of who you are.

#theCOURAGEcode

Because authenticity isn't a liability. It's your loudest and most powerful truth. And it's what makes people follow *you*— not your title.

C

COURAGE in Action: Turn Your Insights into Impact

Activate – Identify one area where you're holding back your true self and commit to showing up more authentically this week.

Elevate – Lead by example: Openly share a personal story or value in a professional setting to inspire trust and connection.

Accelerate – Build a culture of authenticity within your team, home, and social life by encouraging open dialogue and fostering psychological safety.

Game Changers

Want results? Take ten minutes and start here.

1. Where are you still performing for approval instead of showing up as yourself?

2. What parts of you have you been keeping hidden out of fear of being judged?

3. What's one story you've never told publicly—but could, if it meant building trust with someone who needed to hear it?

4. What are your top five core values? Are you making decisions that align with them?

5. Where in your life or leadership are you diluting your strengths in order to fit in?

C

COURAGE

STRATEGY NO. 3:

U – Unshakeable Resilience

(Powerfully Navigate Uncertainty)

Strategy No. 3:
U – Unshakeable Resilience
(Powerfully Navigate Uncertainty)

I was blessed with perfect breasts.

Perky, firm, double D's; if I were in that *Seinfeld* episode, you might say:

"They're real, and they are spectacular."

So, when I find a lump in my left breast, my stomach drops.

Faaaaaaack.

I know in an instant what it takes three months, two missed diagnoses, and one very direct physician to confirm:

"Leisse, you have breast cancer, and it is aggressive. You're going to lose your hair, your breasts . . . and possibly your life."

I sit there in my doctor's office, paralyzed with fear. *I can't have cancer,* I think.

My ex-husband is literally getting married today. *(And I bet the* new *wife has boobs.)*

I'm self-employed, single, and raising three little girls on my own. *I can't have cancer—I can't do this.*

But the truth is, I *do* do this.

For the next several months, I focus only on treatment, healing, and making life as normal as possible for my daughters. It takes everything I have, but with the support of my family and by the grace of God, I make it through breast cancer.

There is only one teeny, tiny little problem: Sure, the loss of my hair to chemo is temporary. But the loss of my breasts to surgery—oh mama, that is very, *very* permanent.

I've always assumed that "breast surgery" meant "recon-struction." The entire medical community seems to support this, as if a radical mastectomy is merely the first of many steps leading to Frankenboob your way back to "normal."

But I'm a bit of a nerd, so I do the research and learn that reconstruction can lead to breast implant illness, with fun side effects like:

- chronic fatigue
- memory loss
- and—my personal favorite—*more cancer*

Um, no thank you.

For me, there is only one option: *going flat.*

As a plus-size, single mom pushing forty who *really* wants to find a partner, this realization is *de-va-stat-ing.*

This horrible inner voice pops up to whisper:

Girl, you couldn't land a man when you had long blonde hair and double D's; if you're bald, bruised, and bandaged, who's going to love you now?

Oof. Exhale.

Now, I hate—like *hate*—feeling that my worth as a woman is tied to my appearance. I'm raising three daughters, trying to teach them and lead by example that beauty comes from within, and yet here I am, confronting my deepest insecurity:

Am I enough? Will I ever be enough?

I can't be the only one who feels like this . . . right?

Have you ever felt like you're *just not enough*?

Here I am, stripped of every physical marker of femininity, standing face-to-face with my fear of never being loved for who I am. And I am scared. Really, really scared.

So, I decide to be brave.

I choose to show up exactly as I am and let that be enough. I lead with my light. And when I do, something completely unexpected happens:

Random strangers stop me on the street, telling me I'm beautiful. Men tip their hats and open doors for me. I feel magnetic. I feel special. I feel seen.

I feel . . . like *me*.

But the real transformation isn't in how the world sees me— it's in how I see myself.

I was forced to redefine myself, to reclaim my identity in a world that had always tried to tell me who I should be. And in that reclamation, I found something unshakable: *resilience*.

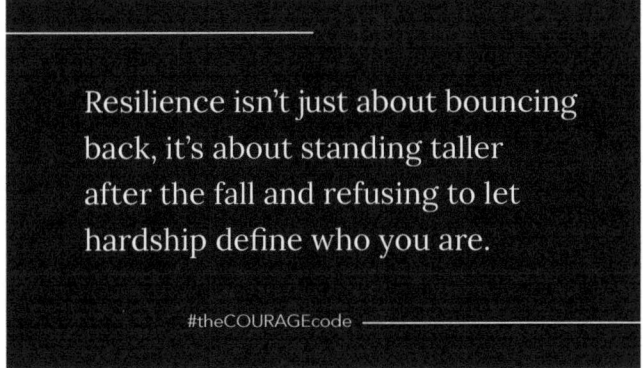

Resilience isn't just about bouncing back, it's about standing taller after the fall and refusing to let hardship define who you are.

#theCOURAGEcode

There is a Japanese proverb, *Nana korobi, ya oki,* which means "fall down seven times, stand up eight." If you've ever been called strong or brave, you know intimately that it's not the falling down part that matters so much, it's the getting back up again. Whether your rock bottom looks like cancer, a failed launch, or a major public misstep, the path back up to the top is *paved* with courage.

The Importance of Resilience in Emotionally Intelligent Leadership

True resilience is about using hardship as a catalyst for growth. It's about taking what life throws at you and transforming it into something meaningful.

We usually mix up the meaning of *resilience, perseverance,* and *tenacity.* So, just so we're all on the same page here, Imma break it down for us:

PERSEVERANCE is *the commitment to keep moving forward* despite obstacles, setbacks, or repeated failures.

TENACITY is *the fierce determination to hold on to a goal or belief,* refusing to give up no matter the difficulty.

RESILIENCE is *the ability to adapt, recover, and rebuild after setbacks,* using challenges as fuel for growth.

Yes, it's a subtle difference, and yes, they all work together like Captain Planet and the Planeteers putting their rings into the middle of the circle to ignite (ask someone born before 1990), but in the COURAGE Code, we focus on resilience in particular because of how impactful it is on leadership during times of rapid change and adaptation.

When I do keynotes and corporate trainings on resilience, I often bring a balloon with me as an example of resilience. What happens after you stretch that balloon out and really test its limits?

It grows.

Leaders who embody resilience don't just survive challenges, they grow from them. They emerge stronger, more grounded, and more adaptable by learning from their struggles, adjusting their course, and keeping going, no matter how many times they fall.

Unshakeable resilience isn't about bouncing back, it's about stretching so you can hold more.

Why Resilience Is the Key to Leading through Uncertainty

Imagine you're playing beach volleyball: the sun is shining, waves are crashing, and if you're lucky, the smell of hot dogs is wafting through the air. It's all fun and games till someone on your team gets smoked in the head with the ball.

Ask me how I know.[17]

Now, we all knew the risk we were taking to play this game, and here is that risk: knocking your teammate—we'll call him Ned—square on the noggin.

Imagine Scenario One: This guy lies on the ground, unable to play any further. Clearly, he is out for the rest of the game, and you need to find someone to replace him.

Night-night, Ned.

Scenario Two: Ned gets up but complains for the rest of the game about his injury, and anytime the ball comes near him, he ducks or deflects responsibility for the ball. He may technically be in the game, but we know he's not really *in* the game.

Now we're all just overcompensating for Ned's inability to handle the pain or to own the injury and step aside.

Scenario Three: Ned takes the hit but gets back up and *locks in*. He is not going to let that happen again. Instead, he learns from this fresh challenge to play smarter, harder, and more aware. How do you feel about Ned now?

My guess is that when this is over, we're taking Ned out for margaritas.

(Which may not be the best choice for a head injury, but . . . whatever.)

The point is this: Life is going to throw you some curveballs; sometimes life is going to smack you in the head and *Knock. You. Down.*

(Find me someone who *hasn't* had that experience. I'll wait.)

Our ability to get back up, regardless of the challenge, setback, or unexpected interruption, is not only what cultivates our own inner well of resilience but communicates to others that they are safe to follow our lead.

Building emotional fortitude and bouncing back from setbacks with grace and grit earns the respect of yourself and others. It's the understated show-don't-tell quality that is so admirable in so many great leaders we know.

Resilient leadership is about handling the inevitable ups and downs without losing sight of the bigger picture. Research shows that resilient leaders share some key traits that help them stay strong in the face of adversity[18]:

- **Adaptability:** Change is the only constant, and resilient leaders know how to embrace it. Instead of resisting shifts in the market, their industry, or their organization, they see change as an opportunity to grow—and they help their teams do the same.

- **Decision-Making Under Pressure:** The true test of leadership isn't making choices when everything is going smoothly—it's staying calm, clear-headed, and decisive when the stakes are high. Resilient leaders don't crumble under pressure, they find ways to move forward with confidence, creating stability for their teams.

- **Emotional Intelligence:** Resilient leaders have a deep awareness of their own emotions and those of the people around them. This makes them better communicators, more empathetic decision-makers, and the kind of leaders who create trust and connection within their teams.

Sounds like you're in the right place.

Why Resilient Leadership Matters

Every time we tune into the 24/7/365 news cycle—accidentally or on purpose—we are confronted with something along the lines of living "in times of unprecedented change." Depending on the social media platforms you subscribe to, you might see this as "living in a dumpster fire."

So, what I am about to say may shock you: *We are doing better than ever before.*

Despite the 24/7 doom-scroll, we're actually making progress. Real progress. In key metrics like poverty reduction, health improvements, educational advancements, and technological connectivity, the charts keep going up.

That's where resilient leadership comes in—to keep us moving forward even when it feels like we're going backward.

The harsh reality is that we live in a *near constant state* of VUCA (volatility, uncertainty, complexity, ambiguity); the very nature of being human, and living in a global economy *governed* by humans, means there is chaos now, there was chaos before, and there will be chaos to come.

Most recently, being in the heart of the AI Revolution and experiencing the *massive* impact it is having on the future of work, leadership isn't just about making decisions, it's about navigating uncertainty, bouncing back from setbacks, and staying steady when everything else feels like it's shifting.

Now more than ever, **the ability to lead with resilience isn't just a nice-to-have, it's essential for long-term success.**

Leaders who can roll with the punches, pivot when needed, and bring their teams along with them are the ones who create thriving, future-proof organizations.

The Ripple Effect of Resilient Leadership

When a leader is resilient, the entire team benefits. Studies have shown that resilient leadership leads to greater employee engagement, increased productivity, and a culture that embraces innovation.[19]

When times get tough, a resilient leader can be the difference between an organization that flounders and one that finds new ways to succeed.

The Challenges and Opportunities of Resilient Leadership

Let's be real: leading through uncertainty isn't easy. From rapid technological shifts to economic turbulence, today's leaders face a constant barrage of challenges. But the best leaders don't just survive these challenges, they use them to fuel growth. They adapt, inspire, and create new paths forward, even when the road ahead is unclear.

The "Burden" of Independence – What Resilience Is Not

This isn't a call to keep pushing through or to "fake it till you make it." Especially for women in male-dominated industries, there's a tendency to treat resilience like just another burden to carry—another way to prove you can handle everything.

Take my client Cara. She returned to her executive role just weeks after her husband's passing, insisting she was fine and determined to do it all. On the surface, it looked like strength. In truth, she was grieving deeply—and struggling. Instead of receiving support, she was handed a performance improvement plan.

I'm not here to advocate for martyrdom. Knowing your limits and asking for help is not weakness—it's a courageous, emotionally intelligent act of leadership.

Resilience, when practiced with boundaries, is not about survival. It's your greatest asset—for impact, for influence, and for truly sustainable success.

How to Build Resilience as a Leader

Resilience isn't something you're just born with, however. Like every other strategy in the COURAGE Code, it's a skill you choose to build.

Developing resilience means intentionally working on different approaches to handle stress, adapt to change, and keep moving forward. Some key ways to build resilience include:

- **Practicing mindfulness** to stay present and reduce overwhelm

- **Engaging in self-reflection** to understand your triggers and responses

- **Committing to continuous learning** to stay adaptable in a changing world

- **Building a strong support system** to lean on during tough times

- **Staying focused on the big picture** to get and keep perspective

Being a resilient leader isn't about having all the answers all the time for all the people—it's about having the mindset, tools, and confidence to keep going, no matter what comes your way.

What Does That Mean for Communication?

There's an episode of *The Office* in which Dwight starts a fire, and Michael—the world's greatest boss (according to his mug that he bought for himself)—runs out of the building first by shoving his employees out of the way.

Not exactly a shining example of resilience or communication in the "inspired leadership" category, right?

We know that resilience is measured in how we show up in the moments that test us most. In leadership, those moments often call for communication: the hard conversations, the uncertain announcements, the change that *nobody* asked for.

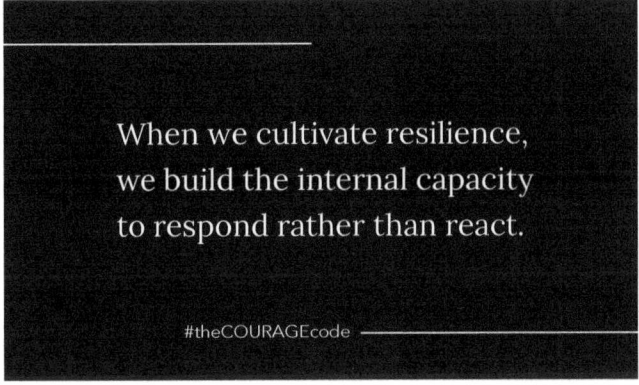

When we cultivate resilience,
we build the internal capacity
to respond rather than react.

#theCOURAGEcode

That grounded presence translates into clearer, calmer, and more compassionate communication—especially when the stakes are high. A resilient leader doesn't avoid the tough conversations, they approach them with steadiness and intention, modeling the kind of emotional regulation that inspires trust and confidence in their team.

Resilience also sharpens our ability to listen. When we're not consumed by reactivity or ego, we're far more able to hear what's being said—and what isn't. That awareness gives our words more weight and impact.

It means we can say less but mean more.

We can hold space for discomfort without rushing to fix it. In a world that's always changing, resilient communication is what keeps people connected, aligned, and moving forward—together.

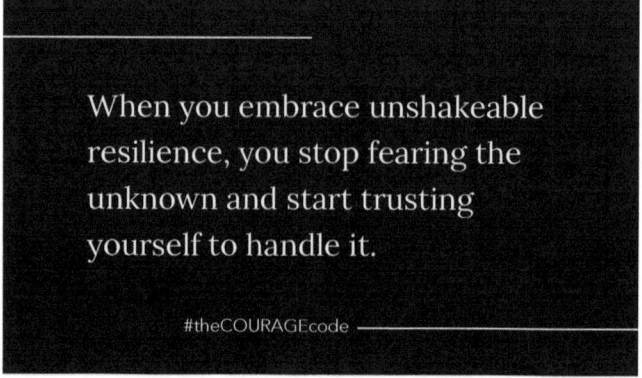

When you embrace unshakeable resilience, you stop fearing the unknown and start trusting yourself to handle it.

#theCOURAGEcode

Because true leadership isn't about always having the answer. It's about standing tall when everything else is falling apart—and bringing others with you through the storm.

COURAGE in Action: Turn Your Insights into Impact

Activate – Identify a recent setback or challenge you've faced and reflect on how you responded. Did you resist, avoid, or embrace it? Resilience begins with self-awareness, so write out three ways you can shift your outlook to see challenges as opportunities rather than roadblocks.

Elevate – Take one of your biggest challenges and reframe it as a growth moment. What did it teach you? How did it shape you? Share this lesson with your team, colleagues, social media, or loved ones. Resilience isn't just about personal strength, it's about inspiring and empowering others by leading with vulnerability and wisdom.

Accelerate – Now, put resilience into action: Set a bold goal that pushes you outside your comfort zone. Maybe it's leading a difficult conversation, taking on a stretch project, or committing to a new habit that strengthens your emotional fortitude. When the inevitable obstacles arise, remind yourself: fall down seven times, stand up eight. The key to resilient leadership isn't avoiding challenges, it's rising stronger every time.

Game Changers

Want results? Take ten minutes and start here.

1. What's one challenge you've been avoiding that might be a catalyst for your growth?

2. How do you typically respond to uncertainty—freeze, fight, flee, fawn (people-pleasing), or *face it*?

3. Think of a time you came through something hard: What did that experience teach you about your capacity?

4. Where are you still trying to "bounce back," when you might actually need to grow through?

5. What does resilience mean to you now—and what will it mean next time life knocks you down?

C

COURAGE

Strategy No. 4:
R – Radical Self-Awareness
(Get Out of Your Own Way)

Confession: For a long period of time, I couldn't stop checking my phone.

I'd pick it up between client calls. In line at the grocery store. Watching TV.

Hell, I even caught myself refreshing my inbox while *in the bathroom.*

This was not my finest moment.

Every time I checked, I told myself it was "just in case":

Just in case a client needed me.

Just in case an opportunity came through.

Just in case someone on my team needed something only I could solve.

But deep down, I wasn't checking for emails or new leads . . .

I was checking for *validation.*

I had unwittingly created a feedback loop where *being busy made me feel valuable* and being needed made me feel necessary.

But in reality?

I was burning myself out while pretending to be productive. I was chasing a sense of worth through external urgency, while completely avoiding the internal discomfort of stillness.

And here's the kicker: I *prided* myself on being self-aware.

I mean—I literally teach self-awareness. And yet, I had this massive blind spot running the show.

It wasn't until I took a weekend offline at a cabin in the woods—completely off the grid—that the clarity hit. I wasn't just addicted to the hustle, I was addicted to feeling *important*.

Sound familiar? If your calendar is always full but your sense of purpose is running on fumes, you might be hooked on the same validation loop.

That moment cracked something open in me. I realized that radical self-awareness isn't a one-time achievement, it's a daily practice. And the second we think we're above it?

That's when we're most likely getting in our own way.

It wasn't the first time I'd learned this lesson.

Gulp.

When I became a mom, I was determined to do everything right. I was an OG "Pinterest Mom"—before Pinterest even existed. I was hell-bent on being, doing, and saying everything *perfectly*.

I was anti-crib, pro-hammock. I made every meal from scratch, nursed around the clock, and—because I don't know how to do anything halfway—I decided to go back to school during my first mat leave.

And then, eighteen months later, I had twins.

I had moved to the suburbs, bought a minivan, turned thirty, and had three babies under two, all within a matter of months.

Still, I tried to keep the perfection going. I wanted to prove I could do it all—and look good doing it.

I became obsessed with building a community around me (*great*) by hosting parties, running camps to babysit others' kids, and generally overgiving and overperforming (*not so great*).

The perfection was crumbling fast. Through bleary eyes and mascara-stained cheeks, I had to face the truth:

If I wanted to thrive as a person, as a mom—and if I wanted my little girls to thrive—I had to let go of the illusion of perfection.

That season of life taught me what it meant to drop the white-knuckled grip on doing it all and instead embrace good *enough*.

It was not easy.

However.

When I gave myself permission to do things like—*gasp*—buy pre-made applesauce and boxed cake mix, it was more than just convenience. It was a moment of liberation. Each shortcut was a declaration: I no longer needed to perform perfection. I could just be *me*.

Which was more than enough.

Identifying and Overcoming the Patterns That Hold You Back

Based on twenty-plus years of working with, for, and around hyper-independent overachievers (and forty-plus years of being one *#facepalm*), here's what I know:

The thing that holds us back from moving forward is us.

Oof.

> The thing that holds us back from
> moving forward is us.
>
> #theCOURAGEcode

Tom Brady didn't need twelve coaches while on the multi ring–winning Patriots because he was deficient—he needed them to *enhance his game* even more.

When high-performing leaders and teams hire me, it's not because they don't know what they're doing, it's because they know *they have blind spots they can't see.*

They want someone to help uncover and interrupt the unconscious patterns that are quietly sabotaging their success and keeping them small, or unfulfilling their potential.

Even the most self-aware of us have patterns we fall back on—deeply wired habits we learned to keep ourselves safe.

They worked *then.* They don't work *now.*

Eighty-five percent of the world's population continues on in life with these blind spots, unaware of how they hold themselves back from having, doing, and *being* what they want.

That explains so much, doesn't it?

You, though—you're in the 15 percent who refuses to stagnate. Who's committed to growth not to be *the* best, but to be *your* best.

(Cuts to me slow clapping for you.)

SELF SABOTAGE

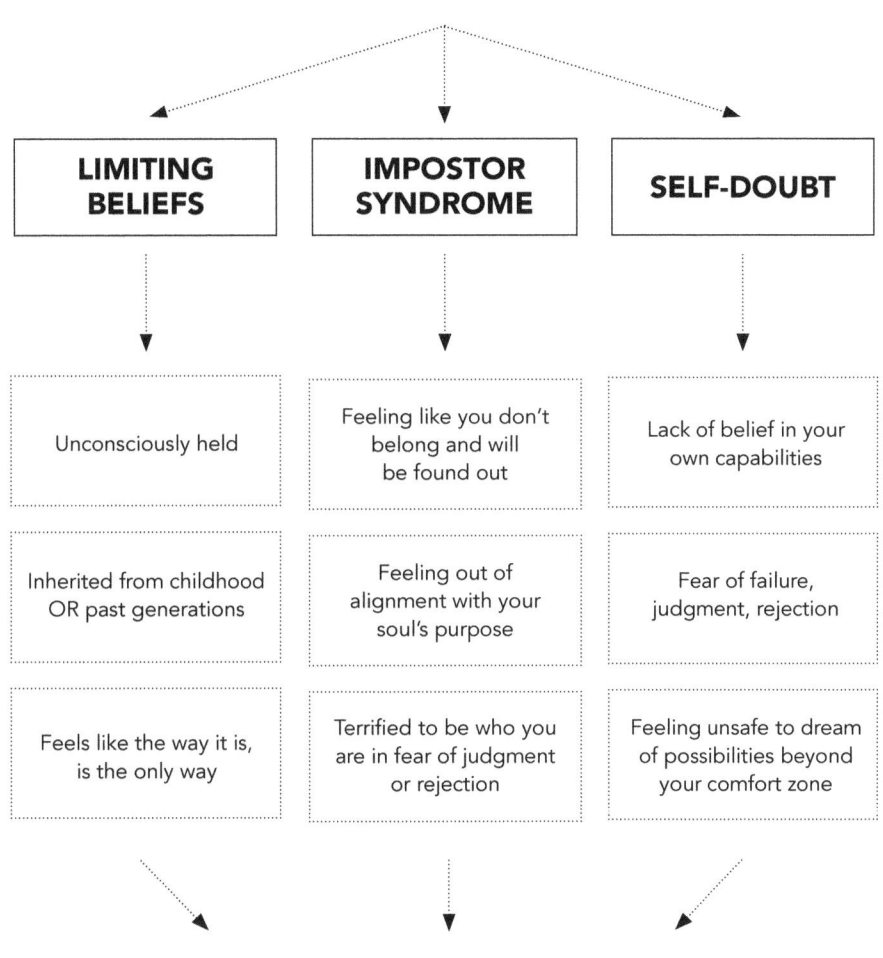

LIMITING BELIEFS	IMPOSTOR SYNDROME	SELF-DOUBT
Unconsciously held	Feeling like you don't belong and will be found out	Lack of belief in your own capabilities
Inherited from childhood OR past generations	Feeling out of alignment with your soul's purpose	Fear of failure, judgment, rejection
Feels like the way it is, is the only way	Terrified to be who you are in fear of judgment or rejection	Feeling unsafe to dream of possibilities beyond your comfort zone

Staying stuck, trapped,
playing small

@leissewilcox

The 5 P's of Self-Sabotage

Ever heard of "the comfort zone?"

Not just the bank-sponsored seats at your favorite pro sports game—your *actual* comfort zone. The place where everything feels familiar, where your nervous system can predict what's coming, even if what's coming . . . kind of sucks.

The reason behavior change is *so* hard is because we are wired to avoid discomfort at all costs. Our brains literally perceive discomfort—or doing something new—as a threat. Which means any attempt to grow activates the alarms.

Enter: The 5 P's of Self-Sabotage.

- **Perfectionism**
- **Procrastination**
- **People-Pleasing**
- **Performance Anxiety**
- **Paralysis**

These are your brain's greatest hits—your go-to behaviors the moment you try to expand beyond what's familiar. These are the tools of your self-sabotage, and they're *incredibly* effective at keeping you stuck.

PATTERN	WHAT IT IS	WHERE IT COMES FROM	SOLUTION
Perfectionism	The need to prove your worth	Growing up being told you're never enough **or** that you're the cat's pajamas—either proving you're worthy *or* maintaining an impossible standard	Balance high standards with realistic, achievable goals
Procrastination	The need to never fail	Avoiding failure by delaying action or keeping yourself in chaos as a built-in excuse—if I don't try, I can't fail	Use effective time-management strategies and clear prioritization
People-Pleasing	The need to not disappoint others	A learned belief that it's safer to meet everyone else's needs first; rooted in codependency and fear of conflict	Set clear boundaries and start prioritizing your own needs—*"No" is a complete sentence*
Performance Anxiety	The need to not disappoint *yourself*	Driven by internal pressure to meet unrealistic standards; often shows up in "choking" moments, even when well-prepared	Build confidence and develop tools to manage stress and self-imposed pressure
Paralysis	The need to never make a mistake	Overthinking, fear of judgment, or rejection that makes even small decisions feel overwhelming—leads to hesitation and inaction	Practice decision-making frameworks and learn to move forward, even when outcomes aren't perfect

Studies in neuroscience show that the brain's amygdala reacts to emotional discomfort the same way it reacts to physical danger. In other words, your brain doesn't know the difference between "this is scary because it's new" and "this is scary because it might kill me."

Which is why behavior change feels really, *really* hard.

In addition, there is a psychological phenomenon known as the "end of history illusion" baked into each of us that we consistently underestimate how much we will change over time—suggesting that the belief we are "fully formed" is another self-deceptive blind spot that limits our growth.[20]

My favorite Carl Jung-ism is:

"Until you make the unconscious conscious, it will continue to direct your life and you will call it fate."

Knowing your patterns is power. Interrupting them is leadership.

For executives and founders, blind spots don't just cost *you*—they cost your team, your strategy, and your bottom line. Radical self-awareness is what separates emotionally intelligent leaders from reactive managers.

Having the courage to name, de-shame, and reframe your own patterns that hold you back is a powerful tool in moving forward: if you can have the sense to identify what keeps you stuck, you can choose to do it differently.

> Radical self-awareness is the difference between reacting from ego and responding from clarity.
>
> #theCOURAGEcode

Alternatively, if you are too wrapped in ego or insecurity and can't challenge yourself to be real about who you are and how you behave, you will stay stuck in what isn't working to protect yourself from feeling further discomfort.

As a leader, the way you communicate sets the tone for your team—and that tone is often shaped more by what's going on *inside* you than by what's happening around you.

When you're not aware of your triggers, assumptions, or unconscious patterns, they can hijack your communication. But when you are radically self-aware, you can pause, assess, and choose your response with intention.

That's how you start getting out of your own way—and out of the way of connection. Self-awareness creates space between what you feel and what you say.

It allows you to deliver feedback without projecting, to receive criticism without defensiveness, and to engage in dialogue without needing to dominate.

When you understand your own communication defaults—whether you tend to over-explain, avoid, interrupt, or shut down—you can start rewriting those scripts in real time. That kind of presence doesn't just make you a better communicator. It makes people feel safer around you.

And safety is what turns communication into actual connection.

Imagine a team member misses a deadline. Again.

The instinctive response might be frustration masked as sarcasm—"Well, glad you could *finally* get to it"—or a cold shoulder to "let them figure it out."

But a leader with radical self-awareness notices that inner spike of irritation, pauses, then checks in:

Am I reacting because I feel disrespected?
Am I personalizing their behavior?
Am I assuming the worst without asking questions?

With that awareness, the leader can choose a more effective response: a direct, curious conversation that might sound like "I noticed the deadline slipped again—can you walk me through what happened so we can course-correct together?"

This shift isn't just about being "nicer."

It's about removing the noise of your own unchecked emotion or bias so you can communicate clearly, lead effectively, and maintain trust. The more you get out of your own way, the more your message lands with impact—and the more your team is likely to respond with honesty, accountability, and respect.

This is where radical self-awareness becomes even more powerful—because it helps you recognize and interrupt the 5 *P's of Self-Sabotage* that quietly erode your leadership presence and communication. Without that awareness, it's easy to slip into *perfectionism*, over-editing every message until it loses authenticity—or worse, saying nothing at all for fear of getting it wrong. *Procrastination* disguises itself as preparation, keeping you stuck in delay when what's really needed is a clear, confident ask. *People-pleasing* can lead to vague, indirect communication that protects feelings but creates confusion. And *performance anxiety*? It turns every meeting or email into a mental audition, robbing your message of warmth and authority. All of these can lead straight to *paralysis*—an inability to act or speak decisively because you're too caught in your own head.

Radical self-awareness helps you spot these patterns as they arise—not to judge yourself, but to shift out of them. It's the moment you notice you're overexplaining and pause to ask:

What am I trying to prove right now?

It's catching yourself softening language to avoid conflict and instead choosing to be both kind and clear. It's realizing you've been stalling on that tough conversation and naming the fear behind the delay.

These are subtle shifts, but they create a profound ripple effect in how you show up.

When leaders learn to notice the 5 P's in action and re-route them through self-awareness, they begin to speak—not from fear, but from integrity. And that's the kind of communication people remember.

That's what builds trust, inspires loyalty, and fosters cultures where other people feel safe to speak with courage too.

The Senior Leader

Imagine a senior leader preparing to present a new initiative to the executive team.

She's spent weeks perfecting the deck—tweaking the font, adjusting slides, rehearsing every word. She keeps telling herself she's "just being thorough," but underneath it, *perfectionism* and *performance anxiety* are in full swing.

The night before the presentation, she considers postponing. Her inner critic says:

It's not ready yet.
You'll sound unprepared.

What if they ask something you don't know?

Here's where radical self-awareness kicks in.

She pauses and names what's happening: *This isn't about readiness. This is about fear—of judgment, of failure, of not being impressive enough.* She realizes that all this editing and delaying is actually creating *paralysis.* So, she takes a breath, closes her laptop, and says out loud, "Done is better than perfect. I know this material, and I'm allowed to be human in the room."

The next day, she opens the meeting not with a polished script, but with a confident, direct statement: "Here's the concept I'm excited to share. It's still evolving, and I'm open to your questions as we go." That one moment of awareness created a complete shift in tone—from guarded to grounded, from perfection to presence. And that shift changes not only how she feels—it changes how she leads.

The On-Site Foreman

Now imagine a foreman leading a high-stakes jobsite—tight timeline, big client, 400-degree asphalt, and a crew that's been running hard for weeks.

Tensions are high, and one of the newer crew members makes a costly mistake that sets things back half a day.

Oh shit.

The foreman feels his jaw clench. His first instinct is to yell, to shame, to regain control through authority. His inner monologue flares up with:

This kid's useless.

I should've just done it myself.
If we miss this deadline, it's on me.

But here's where radical self-awareness kicks in.

He catches himself—just long enough to pause.

He notices the spike in frustration and names it: *This is about pressure, not incompetence.*

I'm afraid of looking like I don't have control.

That's what's really driving this reaction.

Instead of lashing out, he walks over calmly and says, "We've got a setback. Let's talk about what happened and how we fix it together. Mistakes happen—but we don't ignore them, and we don't repeat them."

That one choice—to respond with presence instead of reacting from fear—sets the tone for everything.

The Project Manager

Imagine a female project manager overseeing a large commercial build:

She's the only woman in a leadership role on site, and every day comes with the added pressure of having to prove—again—that she belongs there.

When a subcontractor misses a key install deadline, it throws off the entire schedule.

She feels the heat rise in her chest. Her instinct is to double-check every task, micromanage her team, and silently take the blame so no one else questions her authority. Her inner voice says:

You can't afford to make a mistake.

They're already waiting for you to slip up.

If you don't fix this right now, it's your reputation on the line.

Here's where radical self-awareness kicks in.

She recognizes the signs—perfectionism, people-pleasing, performance anxiety—all colliding at once. She takes a moment, steps outside the trailer, and reminds herself: *This isn't about failure. It's about fear—of being judged, dismissed, or not taken seriously.*

So, she shifts.

Instead of trying to quietly carry the weight alone, she brings the team together and says, "We've hit a delay, and I want full visibility on where we are and how we pivot. I'm not here to point fingers—I'm here to lead us forward."

That one act of naming what's real, and choosing to respond with clarity instead of fear, changes everything. It reinforces her authority, not through control but through calm confidence.

And it signals to everyone on that site—especially the next woman watching—that there's more than one way to lead.

That's radical self-awareness in action.

Not performance. Not perfection. Presence.

It builds trust. It models emotional intelligence in action.

> Being radically self-aware allows you to stop sabotaging your impact and start leading with clarity and intention.
>
> #theCOURAGEcode

And it reinforces a culture where people take ownership—not because they're afraid—but because they feel respected.

That's the shift. From perfectionism to presence. From control to connection. From reactivity to real leadership.

Try This:

Think of a recent moment when you held back from saying what you really meant—or over-explained, avoided, delayed, or sugar-coated your message. Which of the 5 P's was driving the bus? Was it perfectionism? People-pleasing? Paralysis?

Now rewind that moment with radical self-awareness. What could you have *noticed* in yourself sooner? What would a clearer, more courageous version of that conversation have sounded like?

Write it down. Speak it out loud. Then commit to catching the pattern next time—not with judgment, but with curiosity. Because every time you get out of your own way, your voice gets stronger.

And your leadership becomes unmistakably yours.

> Radical self-awareness is not about fixing yourself—it's about freeing yourself.
>
> #theCOURAGEcode

From the old story.

From the unconscious sabotage.

From the pressure to do it all, perfectly.

When you finally see your patterns for what they are—protective, not productive—you get to choose something new and finally get out of your own way to get the results you want.

COURAGE in Action: Turn Your Insights into Impact

Activate – Start by identifying one self-sabotage pattern that tends to show up when you try something new—maybe it's procrastination, people-pleasing, or perfectionism. Ask yourself: *What is this behavior protecting me from?* Awareness is your first power move.

Elevate – The next time you notice that pattern kicking in, pause. Interrupt it with one of these: a breath, a walk, a journal entry, a phone call to a trusted friend. Replace the autopilot response with a conscious choice that reflects your growth—not your fear.

Accelerate – Pick a personal or professional goal that scares you just enough. Commit to it publicly or with someone you trust. Then, make a plan that includes small, uncomfortable steps—and follow through anyway. Growth lives outside the comfort zone. Let this be your rebellion against staying stuck.

Game Changers

Want results? Take ten minutes and start here.

1. **What's one situation from the past week where you noticed yourself falling into one of the 5 P's—perfectionism, procrastination, people-pleasing, performance anxiety, or paralysis?** What triggered it? How did it impact your response?

2. **Which of the 5 P's is your default self-sabotage pattern—and what is it *protecting* you from?** Get honest. Is it failure? Rejection? Not being needed?

3. **What would it look like to interrupt that pattern in real-time?** Think: What pause, breath, reframe, or brave action could shift you toward clarity?

4. **If you spoke with radical self-awareness this week, what conversation would you *finally* have—and how would it sound?** Draft the first two lines of that conversation. Then say it out loud.

COURAGE

STRATEGY NO. 5:

A – Aligned Action

(Define What "Enough" Feels Like)

Strategy No. 5:

A – Aligned Action
(Define What "Enough" Feels Like)

Ken Honda, best-selling author and the "Zen Millionaire of Japan," and his team once did a global study of self-made millionaires. The goal? Understand when they felt rich. Simple question, right?

They interview the first guy and ask, "When did you first feel rich?" His response: "Are you kidding? I'm NOT rich."

Confused, they reply, "What do you mean? You have a million dollars in the bank."

"I may have a million dollars," he says, "but I won't feel rich until I have my own private jet."

So, they go to the next guy. Same question. Same answer: "I may have a private jet, but I won't feel rich until I have a much bigger one."

The punchline? There is no one definition of rich—or even of success. It's all subjective.

A friend and colleague of mine told me that as part of her PhD research, she interviewed twenty-seven women and asked each to define success.

Guess what happened . . .

She got twenty-seven different answers.

That's because most of us haven't been taught to define what "enough" is. And until we do, we will keep moving the goalpost.

During the pandemic, two of my clients were working with me on exactly this. Different personalities, different industries, but the same core issue: not knowing what "enough" looked— or *felt*—like.

Date Night:

Jaclyn was an award-winning musician and mom. When COVID shut down every performance venue overnight, she and her husband—also a musician—were suddenly without income. She felt stuck in the loop of chasing more, always coming up short, unable to maintain the lifestyle they had become accustomed to.

So, I asked her to close her eyes, take a breath, and describe what "enough" felt like. Without hesitation, she said: "It's slipping into a little black Prada dress, booking two seats at the bar of the hotel that burns Japanese plum incense, and drinking dirty martinis with my husband."

While that moment wasn't "in the budget" at the time, recreating the *feeling* was.

She found a little black dress in her closet. We ordered Japanese plum incense off Amazon. She and her husband booked a date night at the kitchen counter sipping dirty martinis they made at home.

And just like that, the spiral of scarcity stopped—because she was able to create the feeling of what "enough" really was.

Lifestyle Loop:

Krista, a serial entrepreneur and mom of two, felt caught in the hustle loop. No matter how much she achieved, it never felt like enough. So, I asked her to close her eyes, take a breath, and describe what "enough" felt like.

She said: "Doing work I love, making my current income, spending as much time as I want at our summer place, and being present for my kids." Then she opened her eyes, stunned. "Oh my God . . . I just described my *actual* life."

In that moment, Krista realized she had enough—and finally gave herself permission to stop chasing more for the sake of it and just *enjoy* it.

Different clients. Different goals. Same outcome:

The freedom from the pressure of more.

Because they finally defined what enough felt like for *them*.

What happens when *you* close your eyes, take a breath, and describe what "enough" feels like?

Because spoiler alert: no one's going to tap you on the shoulder and say, "Hey, hon, you've done enough now; you can just chill."

The systems we live and work within are built on growth at all costs. This means we're conditioned to keep pushing—often without ever pausing to ask: "For what?" or "Why?" The very nature of capitalism is that we are trained to endlessly strive for more—until it breaks us. And you better believe someone is waiting in the wings to profit from our burnout, and/or, you know, *death*.

The reality is that *you* have to be the one to say, "This is enough *for me*." And when you do? You unlock a new way of leading, living, and working.

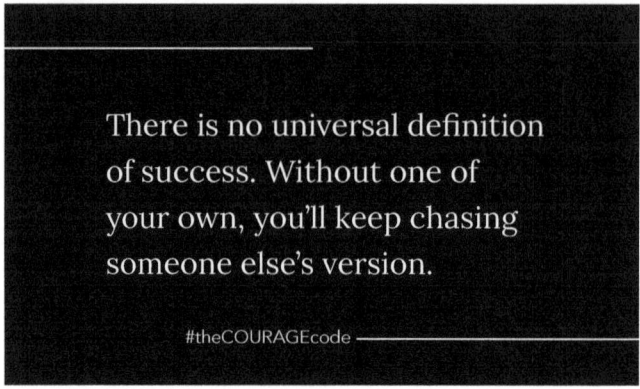

There is no universal definition of success. Without one of your own, you'll keep chasing someone else's version.

#theCOURAGEcode

Defining Success on Your Own Terms

Success is a moving target.

Income goes up? So do expenses.

The minute you get what you once wanted, your brain moves the goalpost toward something you *don't have*.

It makes you wonder, are we really in the pursuit of happiness? Or stuck in the happiness of *pursuit*?

When you stop chasing and start defining *enough*, you break the cycle to start leading from an emotionally intelligent and aligned place of action.

So, how do you *actually* define what "enough" feels like?

Close your eyes. Take a breath. Ask yourself, "If I had nothing to prove, and no one to impress—what would enough look and feel like for me?"

Let the answer come without judgment:

Maybe it's a number in the bank.

Maybe it's mornings without meetings.

Maybe it's knowing your clients respect you, your kids like

being around you, and you get to shut your laptop at 4:30 without guilt.

Write it down. Let it be wildly specific and sensory, like Jaclyn's black dress and incense, or as simple and profound as Krista's realization: *I'm already living it.*

Now here's the shift: Once you define enough, it becomes your internal compass. And *that* becomes a communication strategy.

When you know what "enough" looks and feels like, you stop over-explaining yourself. You stop saying yes to things that drain you. You ask for what you want with clarity—*not apology.* You're not scrambling to prove your worth through more deliverables, more meetings, more noise. You're rooted. And that groundedness shapes how you show up in the room, the inbox, the pitch, the boardroom.

Communicating from a place of aligned action means you're no longer performing or persuading out of fear. You're simply stating your needs, your boundaries, and your vision—with calm, confident authority. And that's the kind of leadership that magnetizes people to follow.

Building a Leadership Style That Aligns with Your Values

Knowing when to stop striving and start savoring is a leadership flex. Aligned action isn't about slowing down, it's about knowing where *you* are going and why. It's about building your work, wealth, and impact around what matters most to *you*, not what Instagram, capitalism, or your old boss told you to care about.

Research shows that people who have a clearly defined internal sense of success experience significantly higher levels of well-being, life satisfaction, and productivity—regardless of income.[21]

Meanwhile, Gallup's 2023 workplace data found that burnout has increased across industries—not from overwork alone, but from a lack of clarity and autonomy.[22] In other words, when people don't know their *why*, they're more likely to feel trapped and disengaged.

I love this Brendon Burchard quote: "If you don't define success for yourself, someone else will define it for you—and you'll be miserable trying to meet it."[23]

Isn't that so true?

Turns out Goldilocks was on to something: we don't want too much, and we don't want too little. What we want is *juuuuust right,* and it's up to us to define it, then action it out in the way that feels aligned.

Whether you're leading a team or scaling a company, knowing your personal definition of "enough" is the difference between building something sustainable or burning out inside it. Only you can define what *just right* means for you, and the sooner you do, the sooner you get to stop chasing—and start living.

And once you've defined what *just right* means for you— here's the magic—you get to *communicate* from that place.

When you're clear on what's enough, your language shifts. You stop padding your emails with over-explaining. You stop saying yes when you mean no. You stop promising more than you're willing—or able—to give.

You start speaking and acting from a place of grounded confidence, because you're no longer negotiating your worth in every interaction.

This is what aligned action looks like in real time: saying what you mean, asking for what you need, and honoring the limits that keep you well.

That kind of clarity is contagious. It creates a ripple effect in how your team, clients, and even your family communicate with you. When *you* model what enough sounds like, it gives everyone else permission to do the same.

In a world that profits from your burnout, defining and communicating your version of "enough" is a radical act of leadership. And the most powerful kind of success? Is the kind that *feels* like your own.

> When you are clear on what enough looks like and can take aligned action, you stop chasing more for the sake of it and start living what actually matters.
>
> #theCOURAGEcode

COURAGE in Action:
Turn Your Insights into Impact

Activate – Take a deep breath, close your eyes, and ask yourself: *What would enough feel like to me?* Write it down. Don't overthink it—focus on the *feeling*.

Elevate – Audit your current life: How much of that vision is already true? Highlight the moments where you're *already living your "enough."* Give yourself permission to notice and enjoy them. Bonus points for expressing daily gratitude for all those things that used to be on your wish list and now you call "your life."

Accelerate – Choose one aligned action to bring more of that enough feeling into your day-to-day life. Book the date. Light the incense. Say no to the extra gig. Do one thing this week that reinforces your personal version of *just right* and sets you on a course of action aligned with your own boundaries, so you can stop living in someone else's.

Game Changers

Want results? Take ten minutes and start here.

1. **What does "enough" feel like for you—right now, in this season of your life?** Describe it using all five senses. Don't worry about logic—capture the feeling.

2. **Where in your life or leadership are you still chasing "more" without knowing why?** What's the story you've been told about success—and is it even yours?

3. **What do you already have that used to be on your wish list?** List three ways you're already living your definition of enough—and give yourself credit.

4. **What's one boundary you need to communicate this week to protect your "enough"?** Practice saying it out loud, clearly and kindly. Then go say it in real life.

COURAGE

Strategy No. 6:

G – Growth Through Communication
(Kind + Clear + Direct = Trust)

I'm sitting at a table of well-dressed women for brunch. I'm in my early twenties, and the impostor syndrome is *real*.

I'm at a swanky French bistro with my then mother-in-law and a group of women who make my annual salary in a *week*—and I'm doing everything in my power not to spill my mimosa.

I am so young, and so wrapped up in my own limiting beliefs and people-pleasing tendencies, that what happens next blows my hair back.

Katrina, a leadership consultant, is sitting across from me. Her eggs benny arrives—fluffy, lemony, topped with homemade hollandaise—and she *sends them back*.

My stomach drops. I feel like I'm going to throw up. At this point in my life, they could have sent me a half-eaten fish and I would've smiled, eaten it, and thanked the server for the privilege.

But not Katrina.

She looks at her plate and says, kindly and calmly: "Pardon me? This isn't what I ordered; could you ask them to send it out with a soft poach instead please? Thanks so much."

No shame. No drama. No guilt. Just clarity.

She got what she wanted using kindness and facts—not frustration, power dynamics, over-apologizing, or emotional gymnastics.

She just asked.

That moment lodged itself in my brain like a seed, and it's grown into one of the most important lessons in communication I've ever learned:

You don't have to choose between being kind or being clear. You can be both.

At the time, I believed in the false dichotomy so many of us are taught:

You're either passive or aggressive.

You get walked on, or you walk all over others.

You're "mean" or "nice."

But that's just not how effective communication—or leadership—actually works.

Most of us aren't taught how to communicate with emotional intelligence. If you're lucky enough to grow up in a family that models it, you're *light years* ahead.

The rest of us are left to figure it out the hard way: over-apologizing, people-pleasing, avoiding conflict, or blowing things up when we've had enough.

Ask me how I know.

Barbara Coloroso, in *Kids Are Worth It*, describes three parenting styles:

- **Brick Wall:** rigid, harsh, authoritarian
- **Jellyfish:** wishy-washy, no boundaries, reactive
- **Backbone:** firm, flexible, emotionally intelligent

Backbone parents—and backbone *leaders*—know how to be kind, clear, and direct.

They prioritize resolution over being right. They lead from curiosity, not ego.

And the reason that matters?

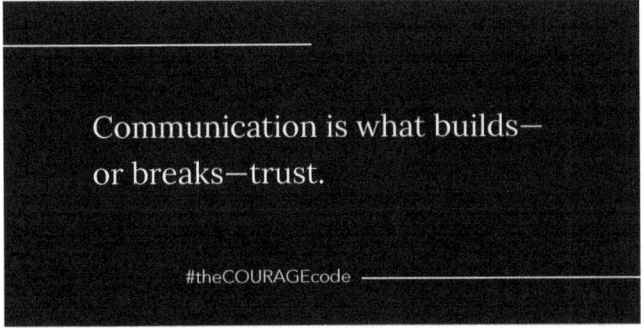

Communication is what builds—
or breaks—trust.

#theCOURAGEcode

If you're leading from a place of needing to be the smartest, the most right, or the most powerful, your people won't feel safe. If they don't feel safe, they won't speak up. If they don't speak up, your whole organization suffers.

But when you create safety by being clear, direct, and kind? That's when people engage, show up fully, and trust you with their best work.

The TACO Method: A Framework for Clear, Kind, Direct Conversations

If you can check your ego at the door and approach everything as already having a solution, you just need to find it—you are very quickly going to build trust, confidence, and engagement from your team . . .

. . . just because of how you communicate it.

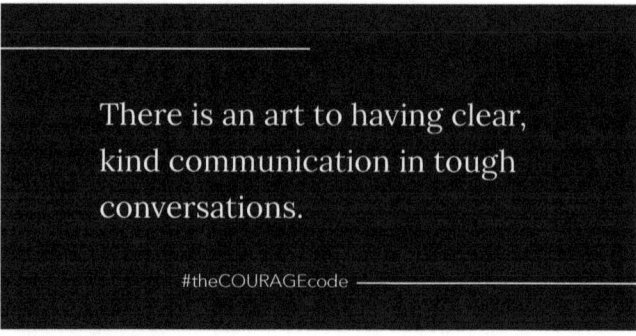

There is an art to having clear, kind communication in tough conversations.

#theCOURAGEcode

This is the communication model I teach all my clients—and I swear to you, it changes lives (and performance reviews) immediately.

It's called the TACO method (*are you surprised?*), and it is the perfect framework to have any (but *particularly* a difficult) conversation. It's so simple it'll blow your mind:

TACO = Timing, Agenda, Clarity in Communication, Outcome Action

01 - TIMING: First, set the date, time, and place. We are not ambushing anyone here, and we are giving two clear options vs. an open-ended yes/no answer.

"Hey, Jim, there's something I'd like to discuss that I think can make things easier. How's 3 p.m. today or 10 a.m. tomorrow for twenty minutes in the conference room?"

02 - AGENDA: Next, be clear on your purpose and intention. This happens in advance. Prepare your intention. Write down what you want to cover and what outcome you're hoping for. Stick to the facts, not emotions, and stay focused.

On your own time, make an actual agenda of what you'd like to accomplish in this time frame. Stick to the facts and exactly what problem you want to solve or issue that needs to be resolved. Include your own desired outcome of what you would love to happen in this conversation.

03 - CLARITY IN COMMUNICATION: When it's time for the meeting, be very clear in how this is going to go. Start and end with gratitude. Be kind, clear, and direct.

"Jim, thanks so much for meeting me here today. I'd love to talk about filing your TPS reports, as I know there's been some confusion about when to file them or not, so I've written down what I'd like to achieve in our time together. I'm hoping to speak first, tell you what I think we can do more effectively, and then I'll hand it over to you for your input, so we can get a clear resolution that works for everyone. Sound good?"

Now you're going to simply walk through the agenda you created, sticking to the facts (vs. being led by emotion, ala if-you-don't-file-your-goddamn-tps-reports-I'm-gonna-lose-my-freaking-mind), conscientious of staying on theme to work toward the singular resolution for today.

So if, for example, Jim is getting feisty and saying things like "Yeah, but Phyllis made popcorn in the microwave and now the whole office smells like popcorn," bring it back with language like "I can see how that would be frustrating; let's stick to the task at hand, and if we need to meet separately about that other thing, I'm happy to schedule it."

Once you've said your piece, you follow through and let Jim do the talking to get his side, again using the above script to bring the focus back, if need be.

04 - OUTCOME ACTION: Wrap up with a clear path forward. Summarize what's been said, check for consensus, and define one or two next steps.

This might sound something like

"Okay, so let me feed back what I've been hearing. Based on [all of that], let's look at what our next step is going to be."

The goal here is to chunk down our outcome into small actionable steps that move the dial forward, and we are doing this together to ensure it sticks. Then we're going to wrap it up with another hit of gratitude.

"Jim, it's been a pleasure chatting with you today. I really appreciate your time and look forward to [actioning out the next steps we discussed]."

Then we go on our merry ways.

Why This Works *Ridiculously* Well

1. It builds psychological safety.
2. It turns reactivity into intentionality.
3. It values everyone's time and contribution.
4. It uses emotionally intelligent language rooted in facts, not feelings.
5. It creates structure and removes guesswork.
6. It reduces defensiveness by focusing on shared goals.
7. It defines success in actionable steps.
8. It turns conflict into collaboration.

Even if the person you're speaking with is . . . a total asshole.

Creating a rough script ahead of time helps you stay grounded, clear, and focused—even if the conversation gets bumpy. Don't read it word for word. Use it as a touchstone to stay in your power: a simple reminder of your intention and direction.

This is especially vital for women working in male-dominated spaces, where being "too nice" or "too direct" is constantly used as a weapon. Communication with clarity and EQ helps neutralize that double bind.

Language-Shifting Tools

Your words shape your reality. Here are small but powerful ways to shift your language for clearer, more empowered communication:

INSTEAD OF:	SAY:
"Sorry for the delay."	"Thanks for your patience."
"I think maybe we should . . ."	"Let's . . ." or "I recommend . . ."
"I'm just checking in . . ."	"Following up to . . ."
"Don't worry."	"You're safe."
"No problem."	"You're welcome."

Why? The brain often skips over negative language (like "don't" or "not") and latches onto the emotional tone instead. Swapping in affirmative language makes your message land with more clarity, impact, and psychological safety.

Remember: You don't have to be loud to lead. You just have to be clear, and kind, and watch the dividends pay out.

A 2024 report from McKinsey & Co. found that organizations with high-quality communication cultures experience

47 percent higher total returns to shareholders than those without.

Leaders who communicate with emotional intelligence improve team performance by **up to 20 percent**, thanks to increased trust and clarity.[24]

Brené Brown really nailed it with this quote: "Clear is kind. Unclear is unkind."

Leadership isn't about who talks the loudest, it's about who communicates with the most clarity, compassion, and curiosity.

And when you do that? You don't just get better outcomes, you get better relationships.

Leaning into opportunities for growth through kind, clear, and direct communication allows you to stop avoiding hard conversations and start creating trust through truth.

#theCOURAGEcode

COURAGE in Action:
Turn Your Insights
into Impact

Activate – Choose one upcoming conversation you've been avoiding. Use the TACO method to map out the timing, agenda, and your desired outcome.

Elevate – Practice saying your script out loud. Edit for clarity, drop any defensiveness, and center kindness. Then, schedule the conversation and stick to your structure.

Accelerate – Start using the TACO method with your team or organization. Your family, your partner. Teach it. Model it. Make it a norm. Watch how quickly trust and productivity grow when everyone's speaking the same clear, kind, and direct language.

Game Changers

Want results? Take ten minutes and start here.

1. **What's one conversation you've been avoiding—and why?** Write out the story you've been telling yourself about what might happen. Then ask: Is that actually true?

2. **How would that same conversation go if you showed up with curiosity instead of control?** Draft a script using the TACO method:

   - When will it happen?

   - What's your agenda?

   - What do you need to say clearly and kindly?

   - What outcome are you hoping for?

3. **Where in your communication are you defaulting to passive or aggressive patterns?** Pick one recurring moment (in meetings, texts, emails, with clients, etc.) and rewrite how you'd say it using emotionally intelligent, kind, clear, and direct language.

4. **What message are you sending without realizing it?** Record yourself having a casual conversation or presenting a point. Watch it back with curiosity: What tone, body language, or language habits could use refining? Where are you already nailing it?

_____

_____

_____

_____

_____

_____

_____

_____

_____

_____

_____

_____

_____

C

COURAGE

STRATEGY NO. 7:

E – Execute with Integrity

(Close the Say-Do Gap)

Strategy No. 7:
E – Execute with Integrity
(Close the Say-Do Gap)

I'm sitting at the bar, trying unsuccessfully to hit on the guy next to me.

None of my classic moves or conversation starters are working—*tough crowd*—so when the topic turns to travel, I decide to bring out the big guns.

I tell him I've always wanted to fly out to California, rent a convertible, and drive the coast up Highway 1.

Even *that* doesn't impress him.

I finish my drink, settle the tab, and call it a night.

But on the walk home, that conversation runs on loop in my head. This isn't the first—or even the seventh—time I've told that story, the one with the iconic dream of heading west, wind whipping through my hair as I cruise the California coastline.

And then comes the uncomfortable question:

Is this something I actually want to do—or do I just like talking *about doing it?*

By the time I get home, I know the answer: I want it. *For real.*

Fueled by two margaritas and a surge of clarity, I open my laptop and book a flight to LA, followed by a four-day Mustang convertible rental.

Within months, I'm driving up Highway 1 *living the exact dream* I used to just talk about.

And that trip? It remains one of the most epic solo adventures of my life.

It also taught me something important: if I hadn't taken action *then*, that dream might still be sitting in the "someday" folder of my life.

That, my friend, is the danger of the *say-do gap*—the distance between what we say we want . . . and what we actually *do*.

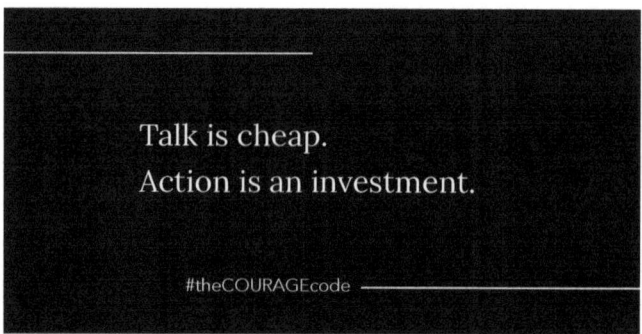

Talk is cheap.
Action is an investment.

#theCOURAGEcode

Action costs time, discomfort, money, and uncertainty—but the ROI in trust, impact, and influence is exponential and always worth the investment.

We all know people who live in the say-do gap:

They talk a big game but rarely, if ever, follow through.

You can hear the same "one day" idea from them for *years*—but they never launch it, commit to it, or make it real.

Leadership doesn't live in that gap. **Leadership lives in our ability to follow through.**

Executing with integrity means doing what you *say* you're going to do—especially when it's hard, inconvenient, or uncertain.

This might be the most important strategy in this whole book, because it's the one that makes *all the others stick*.

(*gets out highlighter)

What Is the Say-Do Gap?

The say-do gap is the space between your intention and your action. It's the moment where credibility is either built or broken.

You say you value rest—but never stop working.
You say you want feedback—but shut down when you receive it.
You say you'll follow up—but don't.

The say-do gap is the leadership version of promising tacos . . . and delivering a sad salad.

Integrity is when your actions match your values. When your follow-through aligns with your intention. When your word is your bond.

Years ago, I worked freelance for a leading online parenting magazine. The founder was a well-known Canadian public figure who was intentional about hiring only women with children for her staff.

She was also very intentional about keeping everyone on as independent contractors, not as full-time staff members.

So, one day when she decided she'd had enough and was going to fold the company, she sent us each an email and/or called us to tell us we no longer had a job.

No notice.
No severance.
No warning.

And no consequence for her.

It was pretty shocking.

More shocking, though, was seeing her moderating a panel *the next day* for International Women's Day, being celebrated as a champion for women.

It was almost comical. ALMOST.

The reality is that this was a shining example of someone having little to no integrity, leadership, or (self-awareness), and a gaping vacancy between what she said and what she actually did.

The say-do gap isn't just a personal hang-up, it's a leadership credibility issue.

The wider your gap, the less trust you inspire. But when you shrink that gap?

You become someone people can count on.

Imagine you're a senior leader who proudly shares with your team that "mental health matters here." You post it on LinkedIn. You say it in town halls. But when an employee quietly asks for a mental health day, you question their commitment or respond with "just power through."

That's the say-do gap.

Closing it? Looks like modeling boundaries yourself.

- Taking real days off and encouraging your team to do the same. Normalizing therapy and flexible hours, or simply saying, "I see you. Take the time you need." That kind of alignment builds trust from the inside out—and it ripples through company culture.

Imagine a site supervisor who tells his crew, "Safety comes first. Always."

It's printed on the hard hats, painted on the trailer, and repeated at every tailgate talk.

But when the schedule slips and tensions rise, he starts pushing guys to skip breaks, rush their tasks, and "just get it done."

That's the say-do gap.

Closing it? Looks like:

- Calling for a proper shut-down when conditions are unsafe— even if it means upsetting the client.
- Telling the new apprentice to take five when they look burnt out.
- Wearing your own PPE properly, every time.
- And being willing to say, "We're behind—but not at the expense of someone getting hurt."

That kind of integrity speaks louder than any slogan.

It earns trust not because you say the right thing—but because your actions prove you mean it. In the trades, where loyalty is built day by day, job by job, *that's* what makes people stay.

It's also not limited to the workplace.

Maybe you're someone with children, and you keep telling your kids: "Family dinners matter." But night after night, you're working late or distracted by your phone at the table.

You've got the right value—but the wrong follow-through.

Closing the gap might mean turning your phone off at dinner. Asking better questions. Listening longer. It's not about the perfect meal, it's about being *present*.

Because when you say something matters and then show up for it? That's the kind of integrity your kids never forget.

And we can't forget being in integrity with yourself, either.

You tell yourself, "I'm going to start writing again," or "This is the year I get serious about my health." But the days pass, and nothing changes.

Integrity isn't just external, it starts with you. When you stop ghosting your own goals and start keeping small promises to yourself—like writing ten minutes a day (dare you to use this book as a game changer) or going for a walk three times a week—you become someone *you* can trust. And that changes everything.

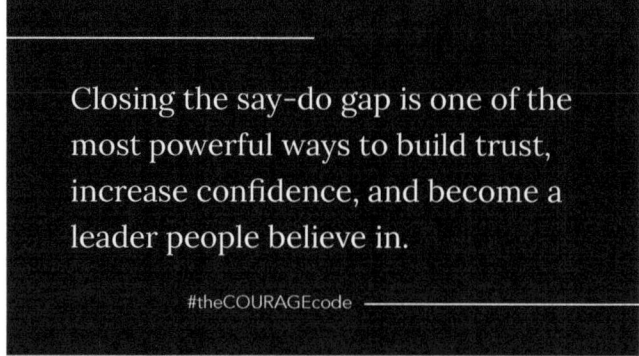

Closing the say-do gap is one of the most powerful ways to build trust, increase confidence, and become a leader people believe in.

#theCOURAGEcode

It's also *really* hard.

Because dreaming is easy. Talking is easy. Planning? You guessed it: also easy.

But showing up again and again to do the thing you said you would do? That is *the work*, and it's where real leadership lives: in our jobs, our homes, and our relationships.

This is especially important when your goals are self-directed—when no one else is holding you accountable. Because if you don't follow through . . . who will?

Emotionally intelligent leaders know this:

Consistency is credibility.

And the fastest way to erode trust? Say one thing and do another.

Let's talk follow-through, shall we?

- Only **3 percent** of people who *start* writing a book will actually finish it.[25]
- Only **37 percent** of people who *start* reading a book will finish it.[26] (If you're still here, you're winning already.)
- In an online learning market valued at over **$185 billion**, only **5–15 percent** of participants complete the courses they pay for.[27]

Why? Because execution is hard. Not sexy. Often uncomfortable. But the ones who *do it anyway*? They're the ones who move the dial, lead the change, and leave a legacy.

Executing with integrity doesn't mean being perfect. It means being *consistent*. It means following through. It means shrinking the say-do gap so small it disappears altogether.

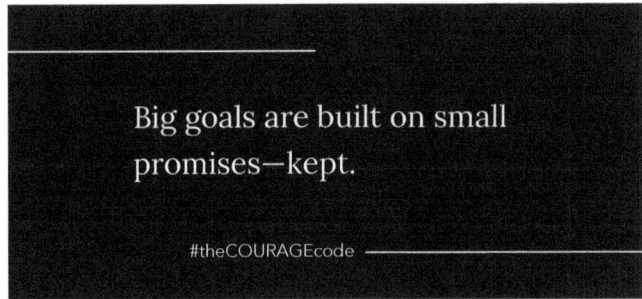

Big goals are built on small promises—kept.

#theCOURAGEcode

When we talk about emotionally intelligent leadership, communication is more than just the words we speak—it's the alignment between our language, behavior, and values.

Executing with integrity is a communication strategy at its core, because the way we follow through *communicates* everything about who we are and what we stand for:

Every promise made and kept sends a clear message: I'm someone you can trust. Every promise broken, even unintentionally, chips away at that trust.

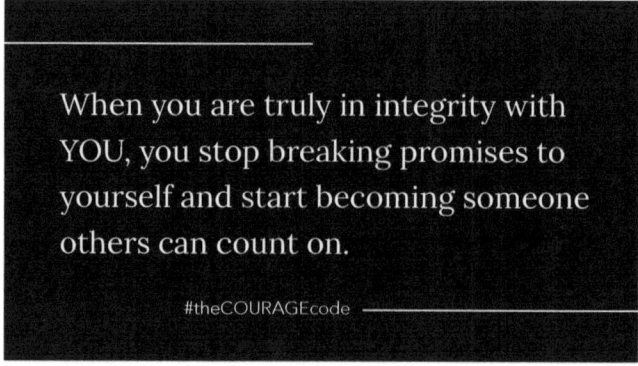

When you are truly in integrity with YOU, you stop breaking promises to yourself and start becoming someone others can count on.

#theCOURAGEcode

The say-do gap isn't just about logistics—it's about credibility, and **credibility is the currency of leadership communication**.

The truth is, most of us don't *intend* to break our word: we overpromise, underestimate capacity, or let discomfort talk us out of action.

#beenthere

But emotionally intelligent communication requires us to become fluent in congruence:

Are my actions backing up what I say?

When you close the say-do gap, your words stop being placeholders and start becoming powerful tools of influence. You become someone who doesn't just inspire with ideas—but leads with action.

And that makes your communication magnetic, because people know you're not just talking to sound smart or look good—you're talking to create meaningful impact.

In a world oversaturated with noise, the most powerful form of communication is consistent behavior. Leaders who execute with integrity don't need to repeat themselves; their actions *speak*.

And actions always speak louder than words.

They create cultures of clarity, accountability, and trust— whether at work, at home, or in their communities. That's what emotionally intelligent leadership is really about: using your voice to create alignment, using your choices to build trust, and using your follow-through to show others how it's done.

Your communication is only as effective as the action that backs it. Close the say-do gap, and your leadership won't just be heard—it will be *believed*.

In the end, *what you do* will always matter more than *what you say*. For execs and founders, your say-do gap sets the tone for the entire organization. For managers and team leaders, your say-do gap sets the tone for how much reliability, efficiency, and respect is mutually generated.

Close your own, and your team will follow. Leave it open, and trust will leak out faster than revenue.

Turn Your Insights into Impact

Activate – Identify one area in your life where your say-do gap is wide. What's something you keep talking about but haven't done yet? Make one small move today toward closing that gap.

Elevate – Commit to a personal integrity practice: only make promises you *intend* to keep. Track your follow-through. Celebrate the progress—not just the outcome.

Accelerate – Invite your team or inner circle into a say-do challenge. Everyone names one thing they've been putting off—and commits to executing it by a set date. Use this as an epic culture-builder for accountability and trust.

Game Changers

Want results? Take ten minutes and start here.

1. **Where's your say-do gap the widest?** Identify one thing you've been talking about *forever* but haven't taken action on. Why hasn't it happened yet—and what would the first imperfect step look like?

2. **What's one tiny promise you could keep to yourself this week?** Write it down. Do it. Then celebrate the act of showing up—not the scale of the achievement.

3. **Who in your life consistently follows through—and how does it make you feel?** Use that reflection to audit your own consistency. What kind of trust are *you* building with others?

4. **What would it look like to run a team—or a life—where your word was your bond?** Visualize it. Then choose one area (home, work, personal development) to close the say-do gap and model that integrity in action.

COURAGE

BONUS STRATEGY: !

(Rest + Joy + Play =
Bye-Bye Burnout)

Bonus Strategy: !
(Rest + Joy + Play = Bye-Bye Burnout)

At the beginning of my coaching career, I became obsessed with uncovering who the big names were coaching celebrities at the top. Especially Oprah. And in my research, I happened upon the story of her longtime coach, Martha Beck.

Legend has it that before Martha Beck officially became Oprah's coach, she had been invited on to the show as a guest for an interview as a life coach.

The production assistant calls up Martha with the exciting news—she's being invited to *The Oprah Winfrey Show*.

(You get a life-changing opportunity, YOU get a life-changing opportunity, and YOU get a life-changing opportunity.)

So how does Martha react?

She doesn't scream, cry, or pee her pants (all things I would unquestionably do).

She says . . . *no.*

Record scratch.

She. Says. No. To *Oprah*.

"Thanks for the invitation," she says. "However, I'm unavailable to film on Tuesday, as Tuesdays I go skiing."

I can *only* imagine the look—and subsequent conversation—between Oprah and her PA.

Apparently, Oprah's reaction was swift: "Get her back on the phone! I need to meet the woman who says no to *me.*"

Long story short? Martha Beck becomes Oprah's lifelong coach. And if I had to guess why, it's this: Martha Beck had the confidence, the ability to own who she was, the unshakeable resilience, radical self-awareness, aligned action, growth through communication, and execution with integrity that someone like Oprah would require to thrive.

In other words? *Martha Beck lived the COURAGE Code!*

And this, right here, is the "!"—our final bonus strategy.

Because every high-performing leader *requires* rest, joy, and self-care to *stay* high-performing.

Rest + Joy + Play = Bye-Bye Burnout

We live in a culture that glamorizes grind and hustle like they're personality traits.

But the truth is, burnout is the *enemy* of emotional intelligence.

High-performing leadership isn't about how much you can carry, it's about how well you can care—for yourself *and* others.

Rest is not a reward. Play is not a luxury. Joy is not a distraction.

They are *the strategy.*

Leaders who build in rest, joy, and play don't just feel better, they lead better.

They model what it looks like to set boundaries, to show up as whole people, and to *not* treat their value as something tied solely to their output.

Let's be real: no one wants to be the person who "used to be a bank CEO" but now has zero identity outside of work, even after retirement.

Or the person who turned their dream business into an obsession and lost all sense of joy along the way. Because as any founder knows, when you do what you love, you never work a day in your life . . . until it becomes your *entire* life.

I feel so grateful to have worked with *countless* leaders who are making it happen. Bringing home the bacon. Having an impact.

And when you ask them what they do for fun?

They freeze. Can't answer. Tear up. Because somewhere along the way, they forgot that rest isn't weakness—it's wisdom.

So many of us pour ourselves into work so much that our job becomes our identity. And when work becomes our singular identity, we start to lose a sense of who we are beyond that title, role, or bank statement.

Joy isn't a perk—it's a power.

#theCOURAGEcode

Together, they keep you human—and make you a hell of a lot more interesting.

And that humanness is what makes your leadership so magnetic, and emotionally intelligent to boot.

And in case you need data to make this stick, I've got you:

- A 2022 Gallup study found that employees who feel burned out are **63 percent more likely** to take a sick day and **2.6 times more likely** to be actively seeking a new job.[28]

- The World Health Organization officially recognized burnout as a workplace syndrome, citing chronic workplace stress that has not been successfully managed.[29]

- Studies show that regular breaks, quality sleep, and play are correlated with increased productivity, decision-making quality, and emotional regulation.[30]

We've all seen this Anne Lamott quote flying around the Metaverse:

"Almost everything will work again if you unplug it for a few minutes, including you."

And we know that to be true. We also know that:

No one is going to give you permission to rest.

No one is going to schedule joy into your calendar.

No one is going to say, "Hey—you've done enough, go play now."

That's *your* job.

And when you finally do? You don't just recover—you *rise*.

I get it: wearing all the hats, spinning all the plates, doing it all at the same time and making it look easy is exhausting.

And for a lot of us—present company included—it's a season of life when we are concurrently balancing raising a career and a family while caring for aging parents, or mourning parents who've passed.

Making rest, joy, FUN, play, creativity for the sake of being creative . . . this is what actually fuels our productivity because it fuels our happiness. *You don't have to earn rest. You just have to allow it.*

Emotionally intelligent leaders know that their nervous system *is* their power source—and that ignoring it comes at a steep cost.

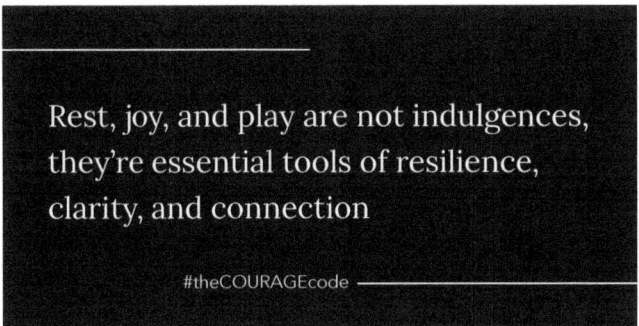

Rest, joy, and play are not indulgences, they're essential tools of resilience, clarity, and connection

#theCOURAGEcode

In seasons of burnout, identity shifts, or major life transitions, the most strategic thing you can do is return to yourself—through laughter, creative expression, and unstructured fun.

Honestly? I've learned this the hard way.

Every time life has asked more of me—whether as a single mom, cancer survivor, founder, or executive navigating the next season of growth—I've had to double down on play and joy just to stay grounded.

It's not easy. It sounds silly to say that aloud, but it's true.

But I've learned to schedule creativity into my week the way I would a keynote. I've learned that sometimes, the most courageous act of leadership is *taking the nap.*

We are not machines—and leadership isn't a performance. It's a relationship, rooted in self-trust and modeled for others through how we care for ourselves.

That means normalizing fun. Honoring boundaries. Choosing joy—not as an escape from pressure but as a powerful way to *reset* under pressure. It's dancing in the kitchen.

It's painting just to see how it feels. It's doing something terribly (on purpose), simply for the joy of trying just for the hell of it. Napping, period.

When leaders give themselves permission to play, they show others how to stay human in high-stakes environments. They model that creativity doesn't require a reason—and that rest isn't something you earn after burnout, it's what keeps burnout from happening in the first place.

In communication, your *energy* speaks before you do.

You can't fake regulated, clear-headed presence—it comes from being resourced. Burnout drains your message, dims your presence, and damages your ability to connect.

But when you're rested, lit up, and living in alignment? That's when your communication becomes magnetic.

People trust leaders who know how to say, "That's enough for today." Because those are the leaders who last.

Emotionally intelligent communication isn't just about what you *say*—it's how you *live*. And when you live with joy, rest, and

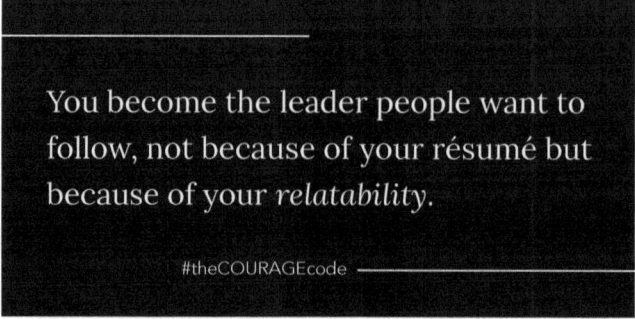

You become the leader people want to follow, not because of your résumé but because of your *relatability*.

#theCOURAGEcode

play at the center, you don't just lead better. You live better.

And isn't that the whole point?

So, go ahead and laugh louder. Take the damn nap. Dance around to the Backstreet Boys in the kitchen.

Rest, joy, and play aren't fluff. They are your leadership fuel. Protecting your energy protects your impact. Stop waiting for permission—reclaim your power by prioritizing what makes you feel whole.

Your nervous system—and your leadership legacy—will thank you.

You stop *earning* your rest and start leading like your well-being matters.

When you reclaim rest, you reclaim your joy, your genius—and your power.

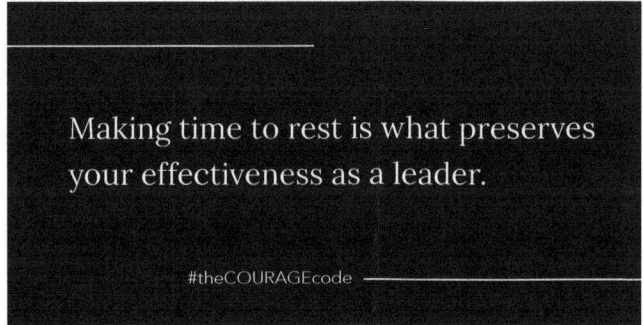

Making time to rest is what preserves your effectiveness as a leader.

#theCOURAGEcode

C

COURAGE in Action: Turn Your Insights into Impact

Activate – Block out one hour this week for pure joy. No productivity, no multitasking. Just play, rest, or delight—your choice.

Elevate – Audit your calendar for energy leaks. What can you let go of, delegate, or simplify to create more space for well-being?

Accelerate – Build a culture of rest and joy within your team. Celebrate "unplugged hours," lead by example, and make space for humans to be humans—not just producers.

Game Changers

Want results? Take ten minutes and start here.

1. **When was the last time you played—for real?** No agenda, no outcome, no productivity hack. Just pure joy. What did you do? If it's been a while, what's one thing you *used* to love doing just for fun? Book it. Schedule it. Do it.

2. **What's your personal burnout warning sign?** (Irritability? Brain fog? Exhaustion? Resentment?) Get honest about your early cues—and decide now what boundary or habit needs to go in place to interrupt the cycle *before* you hit the wall.

3. **Where are you still treating rest like a reward?** Finish the sentence: "I'll let myself rest when _____." Now rewrite it as: "I deserve to rest because _____." Feel the difference?

4. **What would shift if you treated rest, joy, and play as business strategy?** How would your calendar change? Your mood? Your presence at work and at home? What's one new boundary you can implement this week to protect your energy and impact?

5. **What's something you've *always* wanted to try—but haven't because you're afraid you'll be bad at it?** Give yourself permission to do it *badly*. Paint the picture. Write the song. Sign up for the dance class. Try it, not to master it—but to remind yourself that joy lives in the doing, not just the achievement. Start messy. Start playful. Just start.

BONUS: This chapter is your permission slip. If you want someone who gets it, who lives it, who can teach it—book a Zoom coffee with me now at LeisseWilcox.com.

C

Outro

Tuesday has been garbage day for as long as I can remember.

No matter which city I've lived in, it always falls on the same day. Now, when you have the kind of memory I do—the kind that had you seeking out the *one* person in both high school and university who had the same schedule as you because you just *could not keep track* of which class happened on which day in what building at what time—keeping it simple is generally the best option.

The unfortunate thing about Tuesday being garbage day, when you have the kind of memory I do, is that anytime there's a holiday Monday, your world gets turned upside down:

Wednesday becomes the new Tuesday . . . unless it's just a civic holiday, in which case Tuesday remains Tuesday. Maybe I'm overcomplicating things. But hey, I found a solution.

My solution? *Casually look out the window to see what my neighbors are doing.*

Now, I seem to consistently end up in neighborhoods full of older folks, which, in addition to making the neighborhood pretty quiet at night with perfectly mowed and dandelion-free lawns, is a surefire system to know when it's time to take out the trash.

Old people must study the garbage collection calendar because they seem to have a savant-like knowledge of not only when the holiday schedule has changed but also when yard waste, Christmas tree, pumpkin, and autumn leaf collection days are too.

I've learned that if I just look out the window and follow their lead, I'll know when to (*get my daughters to*) take the garbage to the curb.

So, you can imagine my surprise when, on one recent Wednesday after a national holiday Monday, none of my neighbors had put any garbage out. No bags, boxes, or bins to be found.

I panicked: It is Wednesday, right? And yesterday was . . . Tuesday? After the holiday Monday? Making today the new Tuesday? Down is up, up is down . . . I was confused, to say the least.

So, I took a bold step: I trusted my gut and decided to (*get my daughters to*) take out the trash. I led the charge, and figured hey, if I'm wrong, I can always (*get my daughters to*) bring the bins in at the end of the day and try again next week.

And the strangest thing happened: my neighbors followed my lead. For the first time in residential history, I, Leisse Wilcox (*courtesy of my children*), took the lead on garbage day.

I'm not going to lie: it was *exhilarating*.

My palms were sweaty, my heart rate increased, I was not 100 percent sure of what we were doing—but we took the leap and led the charge.

I dare say, it took *courage*.

And while this is a completely ridiculous (but true) story, I cannot stop thinking about how accurately it encapsulates the COURAGE Code.

Why?

Because it takes guts to do things a new way.

It takes bravery to zig when everyone else zags.

It takes heart to take the lead when you're used to everyone else doing it first.

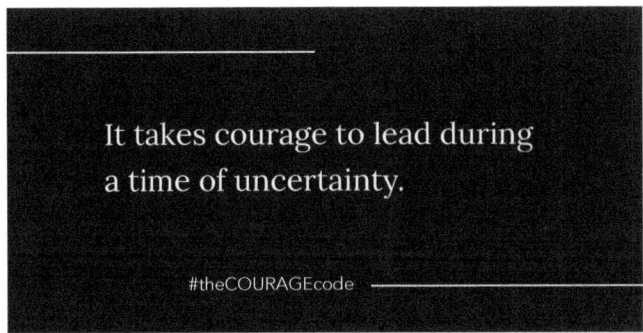

It takes courage to lead during
a time of uncertainty.

#theCOURAGEcode

My dad used to tell this joke about two guys, Bob and Doug, who go camping. They're out in their tent in the middle of the woods, in the middle of the night, when they hear a scratching sound outside.

It's a bear.

Bob looks at Doug, Doug looks at Bob, and Bob starts lacing up his running shoes.

"Are you crazy?" Doug asks. "You think you can outrun a bear?"

"I don't have to outrun the bear," Bob answers. "I just have to outrun *you.*"

AI is the bear scratching at our tent right now.

We're *never* going to outrun it.

But we *can* choose to outrun the guy next to us—simply by adopting new strategies of being in the workplace.

Moving forward into the future of work, emotional intelligence (EQ) is our greatest competitive advantage in the AI Revolution.

Leaders who excel in EQ—those who can empathize, connect, and inspire—are the ones who will shape the future of work. Leaders who can turn that into consistent communication?

They'll be the ones laughing all the way to the bank.

Harvard Business Review identifies EQ as the key differentiator between good and great leaders[31], and global executives at the World Economic Forum agree: EQ ranks as the top skill for navigating the workplace of tomorrow.[32]

Even Jamie Dimon has said that leaders with high EQ will outperform those who rely solely on technical expertise.[33]

Anyone who hopes to not only keep their job but also stay relevant in the new era of work needs to do the one job AI *can't* do, which is to master relationships by excelling at emotional intelligence.

Successful leaders—past, present, and emerging—are going to measure their impact with the measuring stick of the not-so-soft skills that, once considered "nice to have," are now *completely nonnegotiable*.

And while I know intimately that the emotionally intelligent strategies to change the way we work, live, and lead that are laid out in this book are available to everyone, we both know not everyone will "get it."

Many people who've been used to high salaries and the lifestyle that goes with them will find themselves out of work and out of luck because of their inability to adapt and evolve.

All we have to do is outrun that guy.

The faster and more comprehensively we adopt these seven (plus one) strategies, the easier it becomes to be confident, authentic, resilient, self-aware, aligned, fulfilled, communicative, integrity-driven, and emotionally intelligent leaders.

And to be honest? The sooner we do that, the sooner we replace the dinosaur-ic leadership of old and make work a place where all humans can thrive with purpose and impact.

Because the secret that no one wants to share is this: You don't have to be the biggest, brightest, or best. You don't have to be the fastest, most forward-thinking, or famous. You don't even have to be perfect.

You just need to have COURAGE.

Which is exactly what I'm sharing here with you: you have "the code," now use it; change the way you work, live, and lead with these seven communication strategies.

The COURAGE Code.

"Be brave enough to suck
at something new."

–Graffiti beside a Chinese restaurant in my hometown

tl; dr: The World Needs More COURAGE!

- **C**onfidence is a choice, and it establishes your leadership authority.

- **O**wning who you are—(authentic) leaders create environments to get better results from everyone.

- **U**nshakably resilient leaders create a sense of stability by staying steadfast in adversity and learning from past challenges.

- **R**adical self-awareness is the key to moving forward without unknowingly sabotaging your own success.

- **A**ligned action is knowing what "enough" looks and feels like for *you*, so you can *feel* fulfilled while you do it.

- **G**rowth happens through kind, clear, and direct communication that builds trust, fosters safety, and solves problems faster.

- **E**xecuting with integrity means shrinking the say-do gap to build trust, integrity, and momentum—one kept promise at a time.

- **!** Making time to rest is what preserves your effectiveness as a leader.

It takes COURAGE to lead through uncertainty; you have the code, now *use* it.

Ready to put courage into action at work, home, and relationships? Let's keep the momentum going:

Head to *LeisseWilcox.com* to book Leisse to speak at your next event or to facilitate onsite leadership development training for your teams.

Book Club Guidelines: Making the Most of *The COURAGE Code*

This book was meant to be shared. Whether you're reading with your team, your mastermind, or your leadership cohort, here's how to create rich, real conversations that help you integrate each strategy into your life and work:

1. SET THE TONE
Start each session with a grounding question: "Where has this shown up for me recently?" This brings the content off the page and into your lived experience.

2. KEEP IT REAL
This is not about being right—it's about being honest. Make space for real talk, even if it's messy or uncomfortable. That's where the growth happens.

3. USE THE BUILT-IN REFLECTION PROMPTS
Each chapter includes examples and prompts designed to spark conversation. Use them as jumping-off points, or choose one COURAGE strategy to focus on each week.

4. TAKE IT OFF THE PAGE
After each discussion, invite your group to choose *one aligned action* to try before the next meeting. Then reflect together on what shifted.

5. STAY CONNECTED
Leadership can feel isolating—especially when you're doing it differently. Use your book club as a space for connection, accountability, and support as you implement what you're learning.

Book Club Discussion Questions for *The COURAGE Code*

Want to bring me in for a virtual guest spot and guided discussion for your ERG, mastermind, or book club? Head to LeisseWilcox.com

C – Choose Confidence (Permission to Show Up)

- When was the last time you *chose* confidence instead of waiting to feel it?

- What does confidence look and sound like for you in action?

- Where are you still waiting for permission to take up space—and what would happen if you stopped?

O – Own Who You Are (Lead with Authenticity)

- What are 1–2 things people consistently appreciate about you . . . that you tend to overlook or downplay? In what situations do you feel the most "yourself" at work—and what makes that possible?

- Where do you still feel pressure to perform or prove rather than just be?

U – Unshakeable Resilience (Powerfully Navigate Uncertainty)

- What's a challenge that shaped your leadership for the better—even if it didn't feel like it at the time?

- When things fall apart, what anchors you?

- What does *being resilient* look like for you in action—not just mindset, but behavior?

R – Radical Self-Awareness (Get Out of Your Own Way)

- Which of the 5 P's of self-sabotage shows up most for you: Perfectionism, Procrastination, People-Pleasing, Performance Anxiety, or Paralysis?

- What's one recent situation where self-awareness helped you communicate better—or where *lack* of self-awareness made things harder?

- How do you know when you're "in your own way"—and how do you shift out of it?

A – Aligned Action (Define What Enough Feels Like)

- What does "enough" feel like for you—today, in this season of life?

- Where are you currently chasing more without knowing why?

- How does knowing your own "enough" change the way you communicate with your team, clients, or family?

G – Growth Through Communication (Kind + Clear + Direct = Trust)

- Where in your life or work could you be clearer or more direct—*without* being unkind?

- What's your default communication style under stress—and is it helping or hurting?

- What conversation are you avoiding . . . and what would it sound like if you approached it with kindness and clarity?

E – Execute with Integrity (Close the Say-Do Gap)

- Where do your actions already reflect your values—and where is there still a gap?

- How do you hold yourself accountable when no one's watching?

- What's one promise you need to start keeping—to yourself or others?

! – Rest + Joy + Play = Bye-Bye Burnout (The Bonus Strategy)

- What's your relationship to rest? Do you allow it . . . or do you earn it?

- When was the last time you felt lit up by joy or play—without trying to justify it?

- What would change if you treated rest as a leadership strategy instead of a luxury?

Leisse Wilcox doesn't just teach leaders— she *is* one.

As Chief People Officer of a multi seven–figure infrastructure business, and with over twenty years of experience speaking and coaching executives around the world, Leisse transforms leadership by helping you become the **leader everyone wants to work with**.

Known as the "Secret Weapon of the C-Suite" and the "Marie Kondo of Your Unconscious," she helps ambitious leaders cut through the mental clutter, lead with courage, and create workplaces people are excited to be part of.

An expert in **behavioral change, resilience, and high-performance leadership** and certified Leadership, Executive, and Organizational Development Coach, Leisse is an award-winning speaker, twice bestselling author, and *Forbes* contributor trusted by brands like TD, AGF, and Aviva, championing confident communication, resilience, and human-centered leadership that drives results and culture at the same time.

When she's not building the future of work or coaching leaders to own the room, she's road-tripping for tacos, listening to Taylor Swift with her three daughters, or binge-watching HBO with her dog.

Connect with Leisse:
LeisseWilcox.com

in @leissewilcox
⊙ @leissewilcox
▶ @LeisseWilcoxConsulting

End Notes

[1] Graphology, while not exactly peer-reviewed, had its heyday as a pop psychology tool for understanding personality traits through handwriting.

[2] All names are changed in this book for obvious privacy reasons. Client stories, case studies, and anecdotes are shared with permission.

[3] Caroline Picard, "What the Style of Your Handwriting Says About You, According to Graphology Experts," *Good Housekeeping*, January 16, 2020. https://www.goodhousekeeping.com/life/g5057/handwriting-analysis/≥

[4] Nicole Torres, "Research: Technology Is Only Making Social Skills More Important," *Harvard Business Review*, August 26, 2015, https://hbr.org/2015/08/research-technology-is-only-making-social-skills-more-important?

"'Human Skills' Key to Tackling Workforce Disruption: RBC Report," RBC, accessed July 20, 2025. https://www6.royalbank.com/en/di/hubs/now-and-noteworthy/article/human-skills-key-to-tackling-workforce-disruption/jeoz7yh3?

"Automation to impact at least 50% of Canadian jobs in the next decade: RBC research," RBC, accessed July 20, 2025. https://www.newswire.ca/news-releases/automation-to-impact-at-least-50-of-canadian-jobs-in-the-next-decade-rbc-research-677900483.html?

Stephen M. Kosslyn, "Are You Developing Skills That Won't Be Automated?" *Harvard Business Review*, September 25, 2019, https://hbr.org/2019/09/are-you-developing-skills-that-wont-be-automated?tpcc=orgsocial_edit&utm_campaign=hbr&utm_medium=social&utm_source=linkedin

[5] Shelley Thompkins, PhD, "Emotional Intelligence and Leadership Effectiveness: Bringing Out the Best," Center for Creative Leadership, accessed July 19, 2025. https://www.ccl.org/articles/leading-effectively-articles/emotional-intelligence-and-leadership-effectiveness/

"Forget IQ, It's EQ: Why Emotional Intelligence Is The Leadership Skill To Master in 2024," AIMS, accessed July 20, 2025. https://www.aimsinternational.com/news/forget-iq-its-eq-why-emotional-intelligence-is-the-leadership-skill-to-master-in-2024

6. Robert B. (Rob) Kaiser, Ryne A. Sherman and Robert Hogan, "It Takes Versatility to Lead in a Volatile World," *Harvard Business Review*, March 7, 2023, https://hbr.org/2023/03/it-takes-versatility-to-lead-in-a-volatile-world

7. "Survey reveals Canadian employees need more balance and better technology to be productive working from home during COVID-19," ServiceNow, June 18, 2020. https://www.newswire.ca/news-releases/survey-reveals-canadian-employees-need-more-balance-and-better-technology-to-be-productive-working-from-home-during-covid-19-895206753.html

8. Jack Nasher, "To Seem More Competent, Be More Confident," *Harvard Business Review*, March 11, 2019, https://hbr.org/2019/03/to-seem-more-competent-be-more-confident

9. John Dawson, "Why Presentation mistakes are a good thing!" (blog), accessed July 19, 2025. https://www.speaking-infront.co.uk/rethinking-public-speaking-blog/presentation-mistakes-are-good

10. A note on cultural nuance: this is written from a North American perspective and is by no means universal in our examples.

11. Jeff Grabmeier, "Study: Body Posture Affects Confidence In Your Own Thoughts," Ohio State News, accessed July 25, 2025. https://news.osu.edu/study--body-posture-affects-confidence-in-your-own-thoughts/

12. Wendy Rose Gould, "6 Common Eye Contact Mistakes You Might Be Making," Very Well Mind, accessed July 19, 2025. https://www.verywellmind.com/eye-contact-mistakes-8770892

13. Resting Bitch Face.

14. Los Tacos 101 and Casteñada's, respectively, each with multiple locations across the cities. You're welcome.

15. Dr. Josh Axe, "What Is Authentic Leadership?" Leaders, accessed July 19, 2025. https://leaders.com/articles/leadership/authentic-leadership/#:~:text=However%2C%20a%20Harvard%20Business%20Review,business%2C%20gain%20more%20insight%20into:

16. "Is Gen Z the spark we need to see the light?" Ernst & Young, accessed July 19, 2025. https://www.ey.com/en_us/insights/consulting/is-gen-z-the-spark-we-need-to-see-the-light-report

17. Aw, thanks for asking. I have a magnetic head and an uncanny ability to get hit with "stuff" the second I step foot on the court. Irrelevant? Yes. But hey. Felt like the right time to share this fun fact.

18. "The Importance of Resilience in Leadership: Thrive in Times of Change," University of Texas at San Antonio, accessed July 19, 2025. https://www.utsa.edu/pace/news/the-importance-of-resilience-in-leadership-thrive-in-times-of-change.html#:~:text=The%20hallmark%20of%20resilient%20leaders,inspire%20confidence%20among%20team%20members.

19. Courtney Ritchie, "What Is Resilient Leadership? Thriving in an Ever-Changing Business World" learnit (blog), accessed July 19, 2025. https://www.learnit.com/blog/what-is-resilient-leadership

20. Jordi Quoidbach, Daniel T. Gilbert, and Timothy D. Wilson, "The End of History Illusion," *Science* Vol. 339, Issue 6115, pp. 96–98 (2013).

21. Maria del Mar Salinas Jiménez, Joaquin Artés, Javier Salinas-Jimenez, "Income, Motivation, and Satisfaction with Life: An Empirical Analysis," *Journal of Happiness Studies* 11(6):779-793, December 2010. https://www.researchgate.net/publication/225713192_Income_Motivation_and_Satisfaction_with_Life_An_Empirical_Analysis

22. Andy Kemp. "Employee Wellbeing Hinges on Management, Not Work Mode," Gallup, accessed July 19, 2025. https://www.gallup.com/workplace/648500/employee-wellbeing-hinges-management-not-work-mode.aspx

23. Brendon Burchard, "The 6 Steps to Lifelong Success," (blog), accessed July 19, 2025. https://brendon.com/blog/the-6-steps-to-lifelong-success/

24. Ana Crudu & Moldstud Research Team, "Emotional Intelligence in Engineering Leadership and Communication," Moldstud, accessed August 14, 2025. https://moldstud.com/articles/p-emotional-intelligence-in-engineering-leadership-and-communication

25. Marie Forleo, "How to Write a Book (and Actually Finish It) with Linda Sivertsen," (blog), accessed July 19, 2025. https://www.marieforleo.com/blog/linda-sivertsen-beautiful-writers

26. This is anecdotal; industry legend is that a third of books purchased are never read, and another third are never finished.

27. Naveen Kumar, "70 eLearning Statistics 2025: Facts, Market Size & Growth," demandsage, accessed August 14, 2025. https://www.demandsage.com/elearning-statistics/

https://en.wikipedia.org/wiki/Massive_open_online_course

28. Ben Wigert and Sangeeta Agrawal, "Employee Burnout, Part 1: The 5 Main Causes," Gallup, accessed July 19, 2025. https://www.gallup.com/workplace/237059/employee-burnout-part-main-causes.aspx

29. "Burn-out an 'occupational phenomenon': International Classification of Diseases," WHO, accessed July 19, 2025. https://www.who.int/news/item/28-05-2019-burn-out-an-occupational-phenomenon-international-classification-of-diseases

30. "The Psychology of Sleep: Why Is Sleep Important for Our Mental and Physical Health?" Insight Psychology, accessed July 19, 2025. https://insightspsychology.org/psychology-of-sleep-mental-and-physical-benefits/ and https://time.com/5339600/how-to-be-happier-at-work/

31. "What Makes a Leader?" *Harvard Business Review*, accessed July 19, 2025. https://hbr.org/2004/01/what-makes-a-leader

32. "The Future of Jobs Report 2023." World Economic Forum, accessed July 19, 2025. https://www.weforum.org/publications/the-future-of-jobs-report-2023/

33. Daniel Roth, "Jamie Dimon says 2 letters matter more than anything else for having a great career: EQ," LinkedIn, July 12, 2024, Jamie Dimon says 2 letters matter more than anything else for having a great career: EQ

fEMPOWER
PUBLICATIONS

At fEMPOWER Publications,
we don't just publish books—we amplify movements.

We support thought leaders, visionary storytellers, and creative entrepreneurs
in transforming their ideas into powerful nonfiction books, journals, workbooks,
affirmation decks, and personal growth tools that leave lasting impact.

Our mission is to help our authors protect their soul's work, expand HER platform
beyond the page, and turn HER message into a timeless legacy.

www.fempower.pub | @fempower.pub ⦿